Fruits of the Cotton Patch

Fruits of the Cotton Patch

THE CLARENCE JORDAN SYMPOSIUM 2012

Edited by
Kirk and Cori Lyman-Barner

VOLUME TWO

CASCADE *Books* • Eugene, Oregon

FRUITS OF THE COTTON PATCH
The Clarence Jordan Symposium 2012, Volume Two

Copyright © 2014 Wipf and Stock Publishers. All rights reserved. Except for brief quotations in critical publications or reviews, no part of this book may be reproduced in any manner without prior written permission from the publisher. Write: Permissions, Wipf and Stock Publishers, 199 W. 8th Ave., Suite 3, Eugene, OR 97401.

Cascade Books
An Imprint of Wipf and Stock Publishers
199 W. 8th Ave., Suite 3
Eugene, OR 97401

www.wipfandstock.com

ISBN 13: 978-1-62032-986-3

Cataloguing-in-Publication data:

Fruits of the cotton patch : the Clarence Jordan symposium 2012, volume two / edited by Kirk and Cori Lyman-Barner; with a foreword by Tony Campolo.

xvi + 142 pp. ; 23 cm. Includes bibliographical references.

ISBN 13: 978-1-62032-986-3

1. Jordan, Clarence. 2. Koinonia Farm—History. I. Title.

BV4407.67 F1 2014

Manufactured in the U.S.A.

Contents

Foreword—Tony Campolo   vii

Preface—Lenny Jordan   ix

Introduction—Kirk Lyman-Barner   xi

Opening Remarks for the Clarence Jordan Symposium
—President Jimmy Carter   xiii

Part One: *Arts and Storytelling*

1. The Greatest Story Ever Retold—*Tom Key*   3
2. Clarence Jordan and The God Movement —"What's Goin' On?"—*Al Staggs*   7
3. Rooted in the Cotton Patch—*Interview with Ted Swartz*   17

Part Two: *Grace and Healing*

4. On the Road with Clarence Jordan: A Quaker's Journey Toward Universalism—*Philip Gulley*   23
5. Who Would Jesus Bomb?—*Ronnie McBrayer*   30
6. Standing in the Gap—*Dolphus Weary*   42
7. Cotton Patch Reconciliation: Transforming Historical Harms—*David Anderson Hooker*   47

Part Three: *Community*

8. The Kingdom Is Like Kudzu: Koinonia Farm and a New Monasticism in America—*Jonathan Wilson-Hartgrove*   61
9. Tearing Down Walls—*Shane Claiborne*   68

Contents

Part Four: *Agriculture, Housing, and Stewardship*

10   Koinonia Farm and the Permaculture Movement
     —*Wayne Weiseman*   83

11   The History and Future of Partnership Housing
     —*David Snell*   89

12   Faster, Stronger, and More Aggressive: Is Habitat Really A Shoot from the Stump of Clarence?—*Joe Gatlin*   94

A Personal Letter from Clarence Jordan to Friends of Koinonia   113

Afterword—Bren Dubay   121

Celebrating the Life and Ministry of Clarence Jordan: A Working Bibliography—G. W. Carlson   125

Contributors   136

Foreword

Clarence Jordan was as conservative as the Word of God, and as liberal as the love of God. He was conservative because he took the Bible seriously and, like an old-time Baptist preacher, could quote chapter and verse to support his vision for Koinonia Farm. To most people in the racially segregated South, Clarence Jordan seemed to be the epitome of what defined liberalism as he called Christians to live and work together in intentional community, embracing each other across racial lines at a time when such behavior was counter-cultural. His model for Koinonia Farm was derived from the second chapter of Acts, which reads, "All who believed were together and had all things in common; they would sell their possessions and goods, and distribute the proceeds to all, as any had need" (Acts 2:44–45 NRSV).

Those who lived at Koinonia Farm were committed to abandoning America's affluent, consumeristic lifestyle, and believed that we all should live simply so that others might simply live.

In the midst of World War II, those who joined with Clarence Jordan embraced nonviolence as the way to resist evildoers, as taught in the Sermon on the Mount. This made them seem unpatriotic to many of their critics. And long before environmentalism was in vogue, they made living in harmony with nature part of what Clarence would call "The God Movement."

Jordan was irked by the ways in which mammon had sapped the church of its prophetic ministry. Fear as to how speaking out against racism and other social injustices would impact their financial security and popularity had led far too many preachers to give a watered down gospel from their pulpits. It is no wonder that so many compromised clergy deemed Jordan their enemy.

The good news is that more than seventy years later the message of Koinonia Farm and Clarence Jordan lives on and continues to grow. All across America, and even overseas, there are intentional communities

Foreword

springing up, drawing to them thousands of Christians, and especially young Christians, who want to live out the radical teachings of Jesus, and be the kind of church that was envisioned by those first-century Christians, of whom it was said, "they turned the world upside down." In the essays that follow, you will meet some of them and read how their lives were impacted by Clarence Jordan and Koinonia Farm. These essays are printed versions of presentations made at the first Clarence Jordan Symposium in Americus, Georgia. I know many of the presenters and I know they are "for real." What follows is a presentation of authentic Christianity.

> Tony Campolo
> Eastern University

Preface

When I heard about Koinonia Farm's vision for the 2012 Celebration and the request that I serve as chair, I did not hesitate. After a twelve-year departure from the original vision, Koinonia Farm had, in 2005 under the leadership of Bren Dubay, returned to its roots as an intentional Christian community. I was inspired and loved what I was seeing.

It was clear to me why a Clarence Jordan Symposium would be one of the major events of the Celebration. Those at the farm knew the history and the legacy. They felt an obligation to share them and pass them on to future generations. Even with the overwhelming amount of day-in-and-day-out work they performed, they had taken the time to water their roots. It only made sense that a Symposium emerge as a new fruit of Koinonia Farm.

Once more, out of a small group of people comes something of tremendous worth. Following the violence and economic boycott of the 1950s and early 1960s, full membership in the community dwindled to just six adults in 1963, but the foundation on which my parents, Clarence and Florence Jordan, and Martin and Mabel England founded Koinonia (from the Greek meaning fellowship, communion, holding all things in common) was not one based on numbers. From the beginning, the size of the community was not the intention of their "intentional" community.

It may surprise some to know that there are only six full members today. They are rebuilding a way of life at Koinonia Farm started in 1942. Some folks believe that in the late 1960s my father turned away from the idea of intentional community. My mother addressed this on multiple occasions during her lifetime and I add my voice to hers: "Clarence Jordan never gave up on community." He explored other options during a particularly hard time, but he always came back to the idea that however small or whatever direction he felt led by God, it would involve living in the way the early church lived—in intentional community. He always returned to the notion of the koinonia and this place called Koinonia Farm. Giving up on community was something that was non-negotiable for him, even in the hardest, darkest days in Koinonia's history.

Preface

So from these efforts come the 2012 Clarence Jordan Symposium and these two books: *Roots in the Cotton Patch* and *Fruits of the Cotton Patch*. Koinonia Stewards Bren Dubay, Norris Harris, Kathleen Monts, Elizabeth Dede, Brendan and Sarah Prendergast, and I sincerely thank all the contributors to these books—the theologians, artists, academicians, peace makers, farmers, etc., who, touched by Clarence Jordan and Koinonia Farm, agreed to participate. Each one spoke eloquently and made the Symposium an event that will not be forgotten by those in attendance. Now you as reader can share in the experience or relive it if you were there.

We acknowledge with sincere gratitude the tremendous job Kirk Lyman-Barner did as chair of the 2012 Clarence Jordan Symposium. He expanded the vision and worked the details masterfully. He and his wife, Cori, served as editors of the two Symposium books. They have done magnificent work.

We thank, too, Kat Mournighan, a supporting member of Koinonia Farm, and Amanda Moore, a novice in the community, whose behind the scenes efforts along with all who helped them assured a joyous and thought-provoking occasion. For all who supported and attended the Symposium, thank you. A special thanks to The Fuller Center for Housing, Habitat for Humanity, and the Bruderhof Community for all they contributed to assure the success of this monumental endeavor.

All went so well that we are planning for the next Clarence Jordan Symposium to be held in March 2017, the year the community turns seventy-five. We are honored to have Jonathan Wilson-Hartgrove serve as chair of the event.

The Jordan family rejoices over the success of the Symposium, the publication of these books, and at what's happening at Koinonia Farm. Come and see.

Lenny Jordan
Franklin, North Carolina
April 2013

Introduction

In a conversation with Koinonia Farm Director Bren Dubay, I learned that the anniversary of Clarence and Florence Jordan's 100th birthdays was rolling around. It would also be the seventieth anniversary of the founding of Koinonia Farm. Intrigued, I suggested that we have a Symposium similar to the Christianity and Democracy conference President Carter spoke at in 1991 at Emory University. As a young student at Pittsburgh Theological Seminary I had the privilege of attending this event and I proposed to Bren that we owed the next generation a similar type of gathering.

Words cannot describe my excitement when Bren liked the idea, and within a few short weeks, our neighbors in Plains, President and Mrs. Carter, agreed to be honorary chairs. Together we envisioned a gathering of people who have been influenced by Clarence, including theologians, activists, farmers, entrepreneurs, and performing artists who would present papers connecting their work to Clarence's life and example. The final celebration would be the publication of those presentations in this book.

Clarence wrote a lot about partnerships. In his famous 1968 letter he wrote,

> It has also become clear to us that as man has lost his identity with God he has lost it with his fellow man. We fiercely compete with one another as if we were enemies, not brothers. We want only to kill human beings for whom Christ died. Our cities provide us anonymity, not community. Instead of partners, we are aliens and strangers. Greed consumes us, and self-interest separates us and confines us to ourselves or our own group.
>
> As a result, the poor are being driven from rural areas; hungry, frustrated, angry masses are huddled in the cities; suburbanites walk in fear; the chasm between blacks and whites grows wider and deeper; war hysteria invades every nook and cranny of the earth.
>
> We must have a new spirit—a spirit of partnership with one another.

Clarence's ideas of Partnership Housing and The Fund for Humanity caused a revolution. They intrigued Millard Fuller, who called Clarence his

Introduction

"Spiritual Father" and who revolutionized philanthropy with Habitat for Humanity. No longer would Christians simply write a check to missionaries doing the Lord's work in far off lands. Instead they would pick up hammers, trowels and caulk guns and do the kingdom work themselves. Indeed, every nail that is driven and every block that is laid in a wall became a testimony to the legacy of Clarence Jordan and the people he inspired.

And Koinonia Farm continues today to ask for help "shipping the nuts out of Georgia," Clarence's slogan for his pecan mail-order business that sustained the farm during the racial boycott. They also do so much more, from practicing and teaching permaculture farming and design, to living a new monastic life of community, and hosting a robust intern program.

Clarence would be the first to say that an endeavor the magnitude of the Symposium is not the work of any one person. Special thanks need first to go to Bren Dubay for not running the other direction when I proposed this undertaking, and for giving legs to the vision which became the Symposium. Sincere gratitude goes to David Snell, President of the Fuller Center for Housing, who gave his blessing to my time and focus on this celebration. The collaborative efforts of the Koinonia Farm community members, Lenny Jordan, and the dedicated staff at Habitat for Humanity International made the experience both professional and profound. My beautiful partner and bride Cori gave amazing suggestions and edits throughout this entire project. Ted Lewis of Wipf and Stock has been a magnanimous coach over the many months of compiling the presentations and I can't thank his team enough for publishing this important body of work.

I love Clarence's translation of Peter organizing the first Christian community partnerships after Jesus was resurrected: "Rock said to them, 'Reshape your lives, and let each of you be initiated into the family of Jesus Christ so your sins can be dealt with; and you will receive the free gift of the Holy Spirit. For the guarantee is to you and your relatives, as well as to all the outsiders whom the Lord our God shall invite.' Rock was going down on other matters, too, and kept urging them on. 'Save yourselves,' he was telling them, "from this goofed-up society."'

Our society is still goofed-up. But I have hope because of the story of the life of Clarence Jordan and the Koinonia Farm experiment. The answer is found in the teachings of Jesus and life lived in partnership with God and community. Millard Fuller once told me that Clarence often prayed for the interpreters of Scripture. It is your turn to interpret this grand story.

Kirk Lyman-Barner, Chair
2012 Clarence Jordan Symposium

Opening Remarks for the Clarence Jordan Symposium

President Jimmy Carter

I know there are dozens of people here who can make a better presentation than I can about Clarence Jordan. I know his children are here, his grandchildren are here, his brothers and sisters and in-laws are here. But I've been asked tonight just to give a few remarks about what Clarence Jordan meant to me personally and to this region of the state of Georgia, to the United States of America and to the world.

I was thinking, as I prepared my remarks, that in a lifetime of existence, there are very few great people that we ever meet. And of course as some of you may remember, I've been President of the United States. I've known some great men: Anwar Sadat, who helped bring peace to Israel and Egypt; Nelson Mandela, who still works with me in a group called The Elders. We visit him when we go to South Africa. But I also remember on an equal basis, Millard Fuller and Clarence Jordan.

I was coming into the theater a few minutes ago and I found a Walk of Fame inscription there with Clarence Jordan's name on it. I looked at some of the other names, and it was kind of ironic because I remember some of the other names who are inscribed in the front were partially responsible at least, or condoned, the bombs, the bullets, and the fires that tried to destroy what Clarence Jordan created at Koinonia. And finally, as you know, during the 1950s, he was forced to begin selling pecans by the mail since his store on U.S. Highway 19 was burned down, bombed. And he developed the phrase, "Help us ship the nuts out of Georgia."

I think in many ways that prediction has come true, because a lot of the nuts that were in Georgia then and tried to burn down Koinonia have been converted by Clarence Jordan into supporters of what he stood for. And I'm very grateful for that.

The first time we ever saw Clarence Jordan personally was the night that my wife, who was a Methodist, joined the Baptist church. We were having a revival at the Plains Baptist Church and just before the sermon began, Clarence Jordan came in because he was a friend of our revival speaker. I would guess that about a third of the people there got up and walked out, because those were times when it was not a common or acceptable thing for anyone to maintain that African American citizens were equal to white citizens in the eyes of our government or in the eyes of God. This was a difficult time for Koinonia.

I later knew Clarence as an uncle of Hamilton Jordan. Hamilton Jordan helped to shape my life. When I ran for governor the first time in 1966, Hamilton volunteered to help me—both he and his future wife, Nancy. He ran my campaign for governor in 1970 and he ran my campaign for President in 1976. I would never have been governor or President without him. I remember Clarence's brother, Robert Jordan, who was Chief Justice of the Georgia Supreme Court. And so I think that the fine heritage of the Jordan family is still present and active in this country and around the world.

Clarence Jordan showed an early courage. As you all know, in 1942 he and two Baptist missionaries started Koinonia. It's good for us to remember that this was six years before President Harry Truman ordained, as Commander in Chief, that all the military men and women would no longer be bound by racial discrimination. I was an officer on a submarine, and in 1948, that had a major impact on my life. I saw the benefits of what Harry Truman did, and it was condemned, not only in the South, but by the Congress and by many others. And what Clarence Jordan did was not only six years before Truman, it was thirteen years before Rosa Parks sat in the front of a bus in Montgomery, Alabama, and before Martin Luther King, Jr., became famous.

It was not an accident that Clarence got a degree in agriculture from the University of Georgia in 1933 and a few years later got a degree in Greek New Testament, a PhD, as a matter of fact. He started, as has already been mentioned, a "demonstration plot" for God's kingdom.

He founded Koinonia on four basic principles: nonviolence; equality of all people; protecting the ecology of the world; and common ownership. I really didn't have much to do with Clarence until I became a member of the Sumter County School Board. But I had been listening to what he said. When I got on the school board, I suggested that all the school board members—there were only five of us then, appointed by the grand jury—would go around and visit all the schools in Sumter County. All five of us, of course, were white. And the others decided reluctantly to go and visit all the schools. We found twenty-three schools for black children. And they were in the basements of churches or in the front rooms of houses. The school books were all handed down after they were worn out by the white students. I remember going to one place out in Archery, where I lived, and teenage boys were sitting on little, tiny chairs about eight inches wide, that were made for little children.

Finally, though, we had to acknowledge that the black children had so many schools because they didn't have any school buses. So we began to consolidate the schools. And we had to provide school buses. But the state legislature passed a law that any school bus hauling African American children had to have the front fenders painted black so everybody would know who was in the buses.

I say these things not to condemn the society in which I grew up as a boy, but just to point out how far things have come. Later, since I had known Clarence and he had helped me with my school board business, I tried to go down and sell him some fertilizer and seed. He said, "Jimmy, I can buy it cheaper than you can." So I couldn't sell him fertilizer, I couldn't sell him feed, I couldn't sell him seed, but they had peanuts to be shelled and I had a peanut shelling plant, so I was very proud to shell Koinonia's peanuts.

Clarence had kind of a quiet resolve. He understood the problems of the school board, trying to deal with the children in a mixed community at Koinonia, both his children and others and African American children. He maintained his equanimity; he didn't join the civil rights movement and its public demonstrations. But he lived the essence of civil rights.

And then he wrote *The Cotton Patch Gospel*, as all of you know. I have a copy on my desk at the Carter Center always. And it was a shock to me, a revelation to me, but now I began to equate the crucifixion with lynching. And I began to bring the Holy Land into Georgia. Those kinds of things were heartwarming, but also stretched our hearts and minds to look on the resurrection and incarnation of Christ not just as an invitation someday to go to heaven, but, as Clarence would say, it was to indicate God's presence permanently with us.

At The Carter Center now, where Rosalyn and I work, we try to emulate the teachings of Clarence Jordan. In 2008 I helped organize what's called a New Baptist Covenant. It's a remnant of the earliest Baptist organization

Opening Remarks for the Clarence Jordan Symposium

in America. It was called a Tri-annual Convention, where all the Baptists came together, both black and white and others, every three years in Philadelphia. But in 1845 that Tri-annual Convention was destroyed because the Southern Baptists decided they did not want to participate and worship God anymore with African Americans. So we resurrected that concept. And in 2008 we began having the New Baptist Covenant meet every three years. And we had 15,000 people the first night in Atlanta. A little over half of them were African American and the others were white. There was never a sense of disharmony or inequality and all during that night, I thought about Clarence Jordan. In 2011 we had another one. We were thinking about the tremendous changes that are taking place, not only among Baptists, but among all Christians. No longer are the churches the last holdouts in bringing about the integration and equality of the races.

I think the permanent, historic significance of Koinonia has been demonstrated vividly by the founding of Habitat for Humanity there, and then later, the Fuller Center for Housing, and earlier, Jubilee Partners were there. The Fullers and Don Mosley, who heads up Jubilee Partners, are here tonight.

In a few weeks, my wife and I will be going to Haiti. This will be our twenty-ninth year working for Habitat for Humanity. We'll be building 100 homes in Haiti to fill out a 500-home village in the epicenter of the earthquake. So I've learned to remember, in somewhat brutal terms, what life was like for me and other Georgians and other Americans, before Clarence Jordan came along—how much life has been transformed, secular life and religious life, because he lived. I'm very proud tonight to help honor this great man.

PART ONE
Arts and Storytelling

1

The Greatest Story Ever Retold

Tom Key

I was invited here to perform *Cotton Patch Gospel* as a one-person show, and that was an incredible opportunity because in 1979 I came here for the first time having heard about Clarence and Koinonia, and the *Cotton Patch* paraphrase. I came here and met Florence Jordan, who was very gracious to me and took me around the farm, showed me the shed and gave me publications and sermons by Clarence. I also talked with Millard Fuller and negotiated the rights to perform a one-person show that I wrote, which was inspired by Clarence's *Cotton Patch* versions. That eventually turned into a musical, with music and lyrics by Harry Chapin, which I performed for years. So to come back to Americus and perform the show as a one-person show at the Rylander Theater as part of the celebration of Clarence's life was a terrific opportunity.

The first year I did *Cotton Patch Gospel* as a one-person show was in 1980. I did about fifty productions of it around the country, and that summer of 1980 I was working as an actor at the Alabama Shakespeare Festival and met a director who introduced me to Philip Getter. Philip bought the rights to bring *Cotton Patch Gospel* off-Broadway. And we all thought music would really be a great complement to this story. Philip was on the board of the Long Island Performing Arts Center with Harry Chapin, the late singer-songwriter. Philip gave Harry a copy of Clarence's paraphrase of Matthew and John and a little audio cassette tape of one of my performances of the one-man show. That interested Harry enough to have him come see me do a performance in December of 1980. His first reaction after seeing it was, "I was born to write the music to this show."

So we began working on it over a period of the next seven months and had a pre-New York tryout in Boston at the Charles Playhouse in June of 1981. At that point, it was called *Something's Brewin' in Gainesville*. That was the name of the first song of the play. It later became *Cotton Patch Gospel* by the time we opened off-Broadway. That July, after we had closed in Boston and just months before we opened in New York off-Broadway, Harry tragically was killed in a traffic accident on the Long Island Expressway. So this literally was the last music that he wrote. Dave Marsh of *Rolling Stone* said he thought this was the best music Harry Chapin ever wrote. It might be one of the few plays that ever got great reviews from *Rolling Stone* and *Christianity Today*.

We ran from 1981 to 1982 off-Broadway, and I did those performances with an incredible band. Then I went out on the road with it. We ran for six months at the Alliance Theater in Atlanta and then the Dallas Theater Center produced it in Dallas for a seven-month run. Then Dramatic Publishing Company published the script and now people all over the country, thirty-plus years later, are still doing *Cotton Patch Gospel*, whether it's a professional theater company, a tour, a church group, or a school group. It's one of the most-produced musicals in the Dramatic Publishing catalog. I've done, over the years, about twelve different productions, starting in New York and then most recently in Atlanta at Theatrical Outfit where I'm artistic director. We have a theater downtown called the Balzer Theater at Herren's, and I've done it there as well. We won two Dramalogue Awards, which is a national theater award for outstanding contribution to theater.

But most importantly, it continues to have a life, it continues to be produced by so many different people in so many imaginative ways. Some people use it as a fundraiser to raise money for world hunger, which was a cause for Harry. There was an amateur production in Connecticut by someone who had moved to San Francisco after the earthquake. They went back to Connecticut, did a production, and raised $15,000 for the earthquake repair and rescue afterward. There was someone in North Carolina who raised $15,000 for Habitat El Salvador. It just goes on and on and on, the impact and effect that it's had.

I think it's incredibly important and significant, and I was very proud and honored to be part of a Symposium on Clarence Jordan because he was a really important figure. I want to talk about why it's important to recognize him. Often in history, we pay attention to what maybe caused the most attention because of violence. If people had been killed at Koinonia Farm, and they nearly were, maybe this story of what he did here would be more prominent. But the fact that complete violence and loss of human life was missed here does not mean that Koinonia Farm was any less important in the evolution of human and civil rights.

First of all, it was significant that Clarence would use his intelligence and his gifts and his compassion to minister. His background in agriculture and New Testament Greek was employed to demonstrate the nature of a true follower of Jesus Christ by taking a path that is unique and living as Christ would have lived. By that I mean that Clarence not only went to school, but set up a farming community and welcomed people. Most importantly in the Jim Crow South, Koionia Farm offered African Americans a place to work (at a living wage) and live and worship with Caucasians. One of the things that was so jarring was that Clarence would pay African Americans a living wage, and that was a counter-cultural move at the time. Whenever Christianity becomes part of the mainstream culture, or even a subculture, I don't think it is functioning in the way that Christ described, "Your kingdom come." Christianity functions as a counter-culture. So that's what Clarence did by being here, farming, inviting all kinds of people to come and worship together, speaking the truth as he saw it from his studies, praying with these people.

So this life was transformative. His vision, with Millard, was to say that we're going to go to Africa instead of setting up a church; we're going to find out what the people's needs are and we're going to meet them out of the resources that are given by people who are also followers of Christ. That was the seed of Habitat for Humanity.

Any transformation in culture always begins, I believe, in the human person. If it's true that Christ did not die in order to make us Christians but to make us human, I think Clarence is a great example of that. He had the courage to become fully human as a child of God; and his vision is transformative. So this Symposium is an opportunity for people to gather who have been touched in some way or another through his example, through his writing, so that we can further multiply this work. And as long as I'm able, I hope to contribute to that so that on an intellectual level, on an artistic level, and on a personal level. We can continue to grow this vision, which I believe really began 2000 years ago.

2

Clarence Jordan and The God Movement—"What's Goin' On?"

Al Staggs

I was preaching in this big ol' antebellum church, I think it was in Georgia, and I was preaching on that passage from Galatians: in Christ there is neither Jew nor Greek, slave nor free, male nor female, which I'm sure you're familiar with, and after the sermon, an aristocratic, older, Southern woman came walkin' down, marchin' down, shaking her bony finger at me. She had aristocracy emanating from her like honey-suckle. And she said, "Clarence Jordan, I'll never believe a word you say. My grand-daddy fought in the Civil War." I said, "Well, you've got a problem. Either you're going to follow your grand-daddy or you're going to follow Jesus Christ. It's your choice."

I recall another situation, I think it was the Grand Dragon of the Ku Klux Klan of Sumter County gave me a Welcome Wagon visit out at Koinonia and knocked on my back door. He said, "Clarence, you know, here in Sumter County, we don't allow the sun to go down on a nigger." And I looked at him and stuck my hand out to shake his. I said, "You are the most amazing man I've ever met in my life." He said, "What do you mean?" And I said, "A man who has power over the sun? My goodness!"

You know, I have to tell you, when I was a little tyke, we had that song, "Jesus Loves the Little Children of the World," all the children, red, yellow, black, brown. All of 'em. All colors. And I often wondered about that as a boy, because in our county, black people seemed to have the worst jobs, the lowest paying jobs. Black children seemed to have the shabbiest clothes, lived in shanties. And I got to thinking as a little boy, I thought, "Does God have favorite children? Does God love white children more than he loves black children?" Wasn't till I got much older that I realized the problem was not with God, the problem was with us. We love black children less.

Well, that gives you a little background, a little intro, to some of the stories. The stories never end about Clarence and the Koinonia journey.

To give you a little background about my life, I'm a child of the South, you can guess that by hearing the twang—it's an Arkansas twang. I call it a terminal accent; no matter what I do, I can't get rid of it, unless I do some other character, like Dietrich Bonhoeffer or Martin Luther. I grew up in a little place called McAlmont, Arkansas, population 2,000, about fifteen miles north of Little Rock. I grew up in segregated South. My high school class of 1964 was segregated. It wasn't until after that time that schools became integrated. And as a child growing up, seeing what I saw and hearing what I heard in my family, in the community, and even in the church, I can remember what it was like back then. And so I connected with Clarence's struggle, as a white southern male, to deal with the culture of racism, the culture of segregation, to deal with the legacy, if you will, of slavery.

I was drafted into the army during the Vietnam war. In September of 1965 I was drafted and spent my Basic at Fort Polk, Louisiana. I can remember the fear and trepidation I had because about that time a lot of the riots were going on, you remember, a lot of the chaos of the 1960s. I walked into the barracks and African Americans from all over the country were there, and they heard my accent. I could sort of remember soul brothers coming up to me and asking me, "Staggs, where you from?" I gave it some thought, and said, "California." Because you see, being from Arkansas, being white, and being in the army in a barracks with enlisted people at that time would make you very conspicuous. I would like to say I never felt so white in all my life. And I overheard in conversations the concerns of African American soldiers about what they would run into in terms of racism in the military. And I think I began to change ever so gradually about what it meant to be white, and maybe what it meant to be black, and how we were to get along and become a unit of fighting forces against the Viet Cong. How was that going to happen?

This is what Clarence Jordan faced in his time. I want to read something you might remember. "Mother, mother, there's too many of you crying. Brother, brother, brother, there's far too many of you dying. You know we've got to find a way to bring some lovin' here today. Father, father, we don't need to escalate. You know war is not the answer—for only love can conquer hate. For only love can conquer hate. You know we've got to find a way to bring some lovin' here today." You know that song, the lyrics, the song that actually became famous about the time that Clarence Jordan died, at least within a year or two. It was by Marvin Gaye, called, "What's Going On" and it sort of resonates for me with the times of Clarence Jordan, at least at his peak. I think Clarence Jordan really did know what's going on. And that's what separated him from a lot of minister-types. Of course he was not a minister-type. He would have chafed to think you would call him a pastor. He told Florence that he'd never be one of those pastors. "I'm just not cut out to be a pastor." He knew himself well. But Clarence had a great understanding of the New Testament Greek. He was a consummate Greek scholar. And he knew the Scriptures but yet he also had that ability to see what was going on around him, which separated him from a lot of church-types. I think it was Karl Barth who said that good Christians should carry the Bible in one hand and the newspaper in the other. In other words, it's important to know the Scriptures, but it's equally important to know what's going on in front of your eyes in the historical now.

I don't know if you've ever heard of *Biography as Theology*, the great James McClendon book that came out twenty-five or thirty years ago. McClendon focuses on four lives: Dag Hammarskjold, Charles Ives, Martin Luther King, Jr., and Clarence Jordan. It's a fascinating study of how these people, in their own unique ways, lived out theology or created theology out of their life stories, out of being true to themselves. I think that's a very important study.

What Clarence Jordan faced was the paradox between being the Bible Belt South and remembering slavery with its legacy. What a dichotomy! You may remember me pointing that out last night through the character of Clarence Jordan. Addressing the paradox of the Bible Belt, he says, "I think the buckle comes together right about here in these parts," that it's in the Bible Belt where we talk about being saved, being recommitted, being more committed to Jesus Christ, going to church, having Bible study, that it's in *this South*, in this context, where slavery thrived.

You see the dichotomy? It's an extreme dichotomy. And I saw it in my childhood. We went to church. We were fundamentalist Baptists—that's not redundant; there are different kinds of Baptists. We were hellfire and damnation Baptists. I got enough guilt to last me for a hundred lifetimes. "You better get saved before you get out of here or you're gonna die and go to hell!" They painted quite the picture for you. In that extreme pietism, extreme fundamentalist, we-love-Jesus-gotta-get-closer-to-Jesus, it was in that context that we were able to somehow figure out that God loved the black people less, that they were second-class citizens.

There was an African American woman who tried to attend our church when I was about thirteen, and the deacons blocked her way in. In our Sunday school class, I can vividly remember the Sunday school teacher saying there is a difference between Negroes and black people and made the distinction that Negroes are "uppity" people who don't know their place. How did all that happen?! The delusions are deep and amazing. People can believe they're close to Jesus and practice structural and systemic evil at a horrendous level. It is almost parallel to Nazi Germany. There the structural evil, the genocide, and the hatred of the Jews, existed in the context of a "Christian nation." The nation of Martin Luther. The influence of Christianity had been there for centuries.

So Clarence Jordan was having to confront and be confronted by a southern culture that believed itself to be really close to Jesus. And that is the most difficult task of all because once you assume that you are "saved" and close to Jesus, then you don't have anything to tell me. I know the Bible, all the way from Generations to Revolutions. It's similar to when I was a kid. We lived near the railroad track. I brought a friend home from school with me one day and he didn't live next to the railroad track. We were out in the front yard playing ball and a train came by. And he went, "Oh, a train!" And I thought, "Yeah, and there's a tree and that's a house." I didn't hear it—the principle of immunity. And I think what's happened to a great extent in southern culture and Christianity is the principle of immunity. It's like the antibiotic situation: you give children antibiotics so much that they grow immune to it. We have been so saturated in the southern culture with Jesus and the cross and seeing the churches on the county seat square, that we've actually forgotten how to listen anymore. Jesus is not just trying to save "the world" but he's trying to save us!

I think that's what's missing to a great extent: the ability to have a broken heart, to say, "Oh! I didn't know that! I've grown up this way all my life and I didn't see that!" That's why we don't see sexism. We don't see chauvinism for what it is. We don't see homophobia for what it is. We say, "Oh, no, I'm Christian. I've known Jesus all my life. I know the Bible backwards and forwards." So what?! Your attitude stinks. You don't have a Christ-like attitude.

So here's Jordan. Not only did he have a Christ-like attitude, but he had a wonderful sense of humor. I love that! And it's so disarming! It's like the KKK who came to his back door and knocked and said the most vile thing you could say, which was, "We don't allow the sun to go down on a nigger." Instead of saying, "That's a terrible thing to say!" to the KKK, he said, "Why you're the most amazing man I ever met! A man who has power over the sun!" And he often did that. He was so good at that. You couldn't outwit him. It was like the time the Georgia farmer stood up and said, "You associate with communists so you must *be* a communist." So Clarence said, "Well that must mean if I roll the red carpet out for you, I'm a jackass."

How do you speak to the people of God without losing your mind or being hanged from the tallest tree in Sumter County? Clarence was able to find that way, by greasing it with a sense of humor.

Another thing I admire about Clarence is he never came across as a victim. He could have. He could have been a candidate for therapy! On tough days, when I think I have it tough, struggling emotionally or otherwise, I look at somebody like Clarence and I think he must have suffered from loneliness, from feeling that he was a victim of so much abuse. How do you navigate through people who are critical of you, who don't understand, who think they know what you're about and you are suspect and you can't do anything to change it? Clarence was able to live with that stress, that people did not like him. That's instructional, I think, especially for pastors and for all Christians.

The following is excerpted from the question and answer section of the workshop.

Q: You talked about Clarence's use of humor. Clarence himself talked about the "Trojan Horse" parable, and the idea of slipping in under the radar, and making your point. Any comments about that?

A: Yes, it came naturally to him. It was not a contrived humor. He had that old southern charm, humor, that was really innate to him. It wasn't something he had to act out. It was part and parcel of his personality. He utilized it, just plugged it in and used it all the time and it became part of his spirituality, part of his ministerial identity. It was a subtle form of being a prophet. He *was* a prophet.

Q: Tell us how you started the business of impersonating Clarence Jordan and what you've learned in those experiences. Talk about yourself as storyteller using Clarence Jordan.

A. Clarence is one of ten characters I do. The first one I did was Dietrich Bonhoeffer, entitled "View from the Underside," which was informed by my study of Latin American liberation theology at Harvard Divinity School. This is where I started to perform what Bonhoeffer must have seen in prison, how he realized he had been a privileged person and he began to see life in the context of those who were powerless. So I'd done this for years, and some of my best friends said, "We've seen the Bonhoeffer, thank you. You need to do something new." So I began to look around. Who is large enough and would have issues to bring that would be sort of dramatic and prophetic in the same way that Bonhoeffer is? And I settled on Clarence Jordan.

I started doing this about 1989, and it wasn't but a few months after I'd started that Millard Fuller got hold of me and asked me to come to Koinonia for the big twentieth anniversary of Clarence's death. He died in 1969. I thought it was just a gathering of people who liked Clarence, but as we got nearer to Koinonia, the driver said, "Oh by the way, in the audience tonight will be Clarence's grown children, and Clarence's family, and nieces and nephews and the people who knew Clarence first-hand." And I thought, "Thank you, so very much." As we like to say in the south, I died a thousand deaths. So I got up there and there were about 500 or 600 people in that audience; I had only been doing this a few months! But I did it, and this part is really the confirmation, because Jan, the daughter, stood up with tears in her eyes and hugged me. She said, "You don't look a thing like my daddy, but when I close my eyes, I hear my father talking." That was just like God saying, "You're where you should be. You're doing what you ought to be doing."

So I had left the pastorate in 1993 to continue to perform Bonhoeffer and then later Jordan. Now, Walter Rauschenbusch, Oscar Romero, Thomas Merton, Martin Luther, and even Martin Luther King Jr., in some contexts; also Roger Williams and William Stringfellow. Do you see a pattern? These are people who had a unique perspective of what God was doing in their time. They themselves were not "great" in their own time, necessarily. And I thought, "This is what I want to do with my life." I was a pastor for twenty-four years. My next-to-last pastorate was at Portales, New Mexico. I had been at Harvard Divinity School for one full year. If you don't think God has a sense of humor, you're mistaken. I was called to First Baptist Church in Portales, New Mexico, from Harvard. It was as if God was saying, "So you're a high-and-mighty big shot, ain't ya? Let's see how it works out with the Portales people."

They were good people; uncomplicated, and they wanted to know if I could pastor them, which was a good question. What I realized was that I had my heart and head full of ideas studying liberation theology. How was I going to translate that into my sermons? That was a challenge, because I was still watching what was going on in the world. I was troubled by what was happening in the Southern Baptist Convention, the takeover of the Convention, which was in full sway; I was deeply troubled by it. I had a hard time translating it into sermons, because people just don't like you preaching about that kind of stuff. I don't know if you're familiar with Baptist polity, but you can lose your job in a heartbeat just for being considered too liberal, parting your hair wrong, wearing the wrong color suit; reasons don't have to be anything at all. I found it difficult to speak to the issues that were of paramount concern to the world Christian community. They did not want to hear it. So what do I do?

I created Bonhoeffer and Clarence Jordan in order to artistically get under the radar. Art has that ability of helping people hear what they may not want to hear otherwise. Last night's performance was packed with issues. Packed. If I had gotten up and lectured that way, people would have said, "Oooooee!" Bad news on my doorstep. You see, art allows you to say things, to suggest things, to evoke some things, to stimulate some thoughts that you could not do in a lecture or a sermon. I knew there was a lot of work to do. And yet there's pastoring to do, too. That's another thing Clarence had; he had a pastor's heart. He was both priest and prophet, which is the perfect combination.

Q: Last night, you used the words "liberal" and "conservative." You said that Jesus being a radical, a liberal—those words are so loaded with meaning now. I wonder if he would have used those words back then.

A: You know, I'm a southerner. I hear people on the street saying, "That guy's a liberal." That is a bad word. They are saying that guy is dirt, a scoundrel. And I say I'm going to put a different spin on this word. I'm going to set "liberal" in a whole different light. I really do think that Jesus would have been cast under the rubric of being a liberal. You don't really get put on a cross for being a conservative. The powers that be always consider the radical to be a liberal, a trouble-maker, agitator, communist, socialist. And I guess you have to learn to live with that; that you're not doing it just to try to be an agitator, but you have this calling from the Holy Spirit to make a positive difference in the world based upon the ethic of love. But you can't be responsible for somebody's reaction. But how much power do you give that person when they dismiss you as a trouble-maker? Can you go ahead and love them and say that's the way it is with them, and that's how I'm going to be in their eyes?

Q: I remember in a movie, a scene with a bunch of young Nazis, singing hymns to their way of thinking. It was just as eloquent and inspiring as a Christian hymn. I wonder if you've had any experiences like that.

A: What I can relate that to is what I see today manifested in what passes for the Christianity, not only in the South, but particularly in the South. When we were driving here, my wife and I saw signs that said to pray and fast for our country and you'd see a political sign with it. There seemed to be a parallel. And I can say this, because I'm a Baptist, not a Southern Baptist, but a Baptist, but I would say almost 100 percent of those folks are going to vote Republican. And they're certain of it. It's not up for grabs or debate. They know. And I've studied this carefully: Baptists will pass out the voting guides to their congregations, in other words, telling you how to vote, which is very *not* traditional Baptist. Because historical Baptists would say, "You know, we believe in the priesthood of believers. I don't care who you are, you're not going to tell me how to vote. That's between God and me and my heart." But that's what happened in the Southern Baptist Convention.

Many of the televangelists are saying, "We're at a critical time in our country. We need to pray because Obama's going to take us down..!" And I'm thinking, "You need to pray—right! You need to pray!" They need the prayers and you need the practice, to use a Clarence-ism. But what bothers me is that it looks like praise, and prayers, and church, and holiness and all this, and I think, in my view, nothing could be further from an understanding of a God of compassion for all other people than *that*. It's like going back to what I said about the paradox of slavery and the old South. We have a new paradox, and that's this political alignment with the religious right and political extremism. I'm talking *extreme*. You know, there's been some racism going on with the Tea Party and a lot of religious right leaders that has the scent of the old South in it. And I'm thinking, "We ain't moved that far, have we." I see these leaders and these people in church, and they are *so sure* that Romney is God's man, not just a candidate, but God's man. And I want to say, "How in the world do you know that? I want you to go back to your Bible. Don't take it from me, just go back to your Bible." I see a form of racism. And it really scares me.

In the Bonhoeffer play, he asks, "Who are God's people after all? If you say the Jews, then I ask you, why is that so many of his children are being murdered systematically? It does appear that God is standing in heaven with his arms folded in apathy. You may say it's Christians. If you say it's Christians who are God's people, then I have a question for you. Why is it then, that so many of those who usher little children into gas chambers or crematoriums call themselves Christians? Are we God's people?" And that's a good question for us in the church. It may be that God is having a hard time continually converting us from our presuppositions about the way things ought to be. And I think what Jordan was up against.

One of the last times I was here in 1999, we marched down the street in honor of Clarence Jordan. Millard Fuller was standing next to me walking down the streets of Americus and he's laughing! Millard is laughing, just howling! And I said, "Millard, what is so funny?" He said, "Clarence would be just tickled to death to know that we were marching down the streets of Americus in honor of him!"

Isn't this strange? Same with King, same with Bonhoeffer. We want to have the glory. We want people to agree with us. We want to hear people say, "Amen. Yes, that's true." That's understandable; that's only normal and human and it's good when you can get it. That's community. But speaking personally, we sometimes have to be willing to listen to what we believe might be the Holy Spirit. And maybe be willing to live with a bit of isolation; that because of our convictions, not because we want to be different or to be radical, just because of those convictions, that we're willing to stand. "Here I stand. I can do no other."

I'm depicting a man who was courageous, who was faithful. You know, when the economy hit bottom in 2008, I thought it might be time to try something else, maybe be a chaplain or something. So I wrote to two people. One of them was Millard Fuller. I expressed my doubts, that maybe it was time for me to chalk it up, do something else to make a living. Millard wrote to me the most amazing letter in May of 2008. He said, "Dear Al, you know how much I admire you. And you know what I think of your depiction of Clarence. I want to tell you a story. I remember finding Clarence in the shack with his head against the wall. And seeing him, knowing he was gone, my heart was crushed. I was so sad. But then in an instant it came to me: Clarence, you finished the race. You finished the race!"

Then in the last paragraph, Millard wrote: "Now, it's the long distance run we're in. There are bumps in the road, there are challenges, there are struggles, but Al, this is a long haul. We're in it for the long haul."

And just eight months later, Millard left us suddenly. And I thought, "How proleptic. He had finished the race himself. I treasure that letter and I remind myself of those truths when on those days I don't have the applause, I have to sit in the solitude of my room with my thoughts and say, "It's the God-work that I'm in; it's the God Movement, something bigger than me or my ego. It's a long distance run."

3

Rooted in the Cotton Patch

Interview with Ted Swartz

Why are you here?

I was asked to come perform and it's what I do for a living . . . perform. So it's nice to connect my profession with issues and causes I feel passionate about. Some is storytelling, some is what Clarence Jordan stood for and what the people I know in these organizations I believe in . . . I think we are compelled by people we trust and admire . . . the ones who are practicing the doing as opposed to preaching the believing. That's a powerful, powerful message. This is one of the best examples of people that are still trying to do that. You know, picking southern Georgia as the place to start an experiment, that's . . . well, that takes balls.

What was powerful for me this morning was a speaker who said that in regard to Palestine and the resistance, "How do you have the strength to do these things?" The same thing could have been asked of Clarence and his people. "How do you have the strength to do these things?" The answer is simply, "Jesus." That was an emotional experience for me this morning, because sometimes we make it complicated, though it is complex—peacemaking, racial reconciliation—but the source of strength should perhaps be less complicated: Jesus.

Something else I love about the Symposium is that there are—if you count my work that's sprinkled throughout today—four theatrical presentations in a two-day Symposium. That's a significant thing. I don't know of any other place that deals with significant issues using theater but is not a theater conference.

It's about storytelling. It's about stories that people are learning again. Tom Key does the Gospel stories so we're learning *again* that story. I'm doing pieces of biblical stories, and then tonight we hear the story again of Clarence in a form that's going to stick in our heads. Al Staggs's work last night, the stories this morning, even the keynotes, were sprinkled with elements of story—and we all know them. But it takes a certain amount of trust to say, "I'm *just* going to tell a story."

I sometimes talk about it as a pitcher who keeps throwing a fastball; you're going to get the crap kicked out of you. You have to throw a change-up. A change-up means that you throw the balance of the hitter off. So the audience—you give them less so they need to come *to* you to get information. So you tell a story that doesn't give them all the information and the audience is engaged. That's what's so powerful about live theater. It's a celebration of art, story, and theater as well this weekend. That's why I'm here.

Clarence's message was his way of life. How is that the right way to live and how has that been inspirational for you?

Tom Key said it in his workshop this morning, and I believe it as well for my work: it's impossible to separate my work in art from a secular or a sacred space. They're all the same thing. It doesn't matter what the material is. You're living your life within that art form so that the doing speaks to your life. Clarence talked about living a life of "doing." I don't—I caught myself—I almost said I don't believe in believing. But I don't feel that we get anywhere by believing. Getting up and moving; theater has a great model for it: you can't experience something unless your body's involved in it. You communicate onstage with your whole being. Your whole body has to be connected to it. I think we know in our bodies, as we know in our souls, why something is right. Our bodies are speaking to us when you connect to people and live in the right way. That's why when we get inside our heads and it's about belief, we can disassociate, because our bodies are not engaged. But the doing is standing next to somebody of a different color, standing next to someone who *was* your enemy, loving someone, standing up against injustice on a daily basis and putting your body in action and in danger.

Mysticism is not magic; it's when your whole being knows that something is right. And I think that's why the message of Jesus is so unique. It's the only one that I know of that turns it all upside down and says that in order for us to function in the way that God wants us to live we have to love our enemy—you have to *do*. It's Tom's piece in *The Cotton Patch Gospel* last night: "love your neighbor as you love yourself" . . . *that's all I got to say.*

Scott Umstead, Interviewer

PART TWO

Grace and Healing

4

On the Road with Clarence Jordan

A Quaker's Journey Toward Universalism

Philip Gulley

It is an honor to share with all of you today, to celebrate the prophetic ministry of Clarence Jordan. Though I did not have the great, good fortune of ever knowing him, I sense a modesty and humility in his writings, which makes me suspect that if he were still living, he would not be with us this evening. Instead, he would be back at his beloved Koinonia, writing something sure to irritate someone somewhere.

I first "met" Clarence Jordan in 1982, in Dallas Lee's book, *The Substance of Faith and Other Cotton Patch Sermons by Clarence Jordan*. It was in a Christian bookstore in my Indiana town. The owner of the bookstore was a Christian fundamentalist, who had obviously not checked the book for theological purity. Twenty-two years later I wrote my own book citing some of Clarence Jordan's more provocative passages, and that same bookstore owner stood in a crowded church and asked, "Where did you learn such heresy?"

"From a book I purchased in your store twenty-two years ago," I answered. It was a lovely moment. I had been dabbling in agnosticism at the time, but that incident restored my belief in a theistic God.

I was taught at an early age that God's love stopped at the borders of the Roman Catholic church. When my Catholic mother married my Baptist father, both families were appalled. When my grandmother Gulley died, we found among her papers a letter her brother had written to my father, warning him not to sign anything from the Catholic church, that the Catholics had been known to steal children and send them to the pope who turned them into priests and nuns. There were five children in our family. I know for a fact there were days my father prayed the pope would take us.

Then, at the age of 17, I became a Quaker at an evangelical Friends church where the pastor told me he was so grateful I had left Catholicism to become a Christian. And I was grateful, too.

Four years later, I met Clarence Jordan in a book, thirteen years after his death.

"He be gone now," a neighbor of Jordan's said after his death, "but his footprint still here." And let me tell you, those footprints were so clear, so vivid, so inviting, one could follow them all the way to the God Movement.

I read, and reread, then read again, his sermon, "The Father's Pursuing Love," Clarence Jordan's take on the lost sheep, the lost coin, and the lost son. Listen for a moment to this gifted scholar and wordsmith:

> A certain shepherd had a hundred sheep and he lost one. Will he not leave the 99 in the flock to go out and seek for the lost sheep? And when he has found it he lays it upon his shoulders and comes in and says, "Rejoice with me, I've found my sheep which was lost."
>
> Now how long did the shepherd search for the sheep? Until it got dark? No. Until he found it.
>
> What does this say to us about God? Doesn't it say to us that God in his relationship to us is not bound by time or circumstances? Suppose the shepherd had not found the sheep when the darkness of night descended, and the shepherd said, "Well, the darkness has overcome the light and I must go home."
>
> Are we dealing with that kind of shepherd—one who lets darkness discourage him? Aren't we dealing with a shepherd who is not thwarted by the darkness of the night, nor the darkness of the grave?
>
> I am not objecting to as many chances as it takes to enfold a man into God's love that never quits. His love is such a precious thing to me that I covet it for all. God is not a celestial prison

warden jangling the keys on a bunch of lifers—he's a shepherd seeking for sheep, a woman searching for coins, a father waiting for his son.[1]

What a lovely image, and the second I read it, I believed it.

I was working as a youth minister at the time, so I read the young people in my church Clarence's sermon; they went home and told their parents, some of whom also thought it was lovely, and some of whom didn't and urged me to reconsider my theology. Well, you know how it is when you're young. You want the approval of your elders. You don't let on that you do, but inside you want that pat on the back. And you're always a little afraid, when you go against the orthodoxy of the day, that you might be wrong and God will smite you, or give you acne and boils and leprosy. So I didn't say anything more.

I got married, and went to college. My wife lost her job, and we were broke. We were like Mitt and Ann Romney, eating tuna on a folding ironing board in our kitchen. Well, we didn't have a trust fund or stocks, but other than that we were just like Mitt and Ann Romney. Well, maybe not just like them, but we did have an ironing board, so we were kind of like them. And one day, my car broke down. It was winter and cold and raining, and I was sitting in my car alongside a road and no one was stopping and we didn't have any money. So I was sitting in my car thanking God for taking such good care of us, and I had what the psychologist Abraham Maslow called a *peak experience*. It was this ecstatic, transformative moment when I felt deeply connected to God and to all the world. It was incredibly beautiful. It didn't last long, peak experiences don't, but what it lacked in duration, it more than made up for in intensity.

When I hear people describe near-death experiences, it sounds a lot like what happened to me—this feeling of deep, universal grace, suffused with this warm light and loving acceptance. And I knew in that moment that God not only loved me, but that God loved everyone in the world, and was unswervingly committed to everyone's eternal well-being. I knew, in the words of Meister Eckhart, that "every creature was a word of God."

In that moment, I resolved that I would never hold a theology which placed one group above another. That week, I got a phone call from a rural Quaker meeting looking for a pastor, and I agreed to an interview. We met, and talked, and they offered me a job. They said, "Why not, in your

---

1. Clarence Jordan, *The Substance of Faith and Other Cotton Patch Sermons*, ed. Dallas Lee (Eugene, OR: Cascade, 2005), 170.

first sermon, you tell us what you believe." So I gave a sermon about God's universal love, quoting, with proper attribution, from Clarence Jordan's sermon. "*God is not a celestial prison warden jangling the keys on a bunch of lifers—he's a shepherd seeking for sheep, a woman searching for coins, a father waiting for his son.*" Good stuff, right? Except the organist came up to me afterwards and asked if I believed in hell. I asked her what she meant by hell. She said the place people go who don't accept Jesus as their Savior. I said, "No, I don't believe in that kind of hell." Not after reading Clarence Jordan and having my peak experience.

She phoned the elders that week, telling them that unless I believed in hell, she would no longer play the organ at the church. The head elder phoned me and explained what was going on. "The thing is," he said, "it took us six months to find an organist and only a week to find you. We sure don't want to lose her. So if you could tell her you believe in hell, this little problem will go away." I said, "No, I'm not going to lie."

When I arrived at meeting the next Sunday, the elders told me I couldn't preach. So we sat in Quaker silence for an hour, no one saying anything. After meeting for worship, they asked me to meet with them, and asked me again to tell the organist I believed in hell. But I wouldn't do it, so was fired. I went out to the car where my wife was waiting.

"What happened?" she asked.

"Good news and bad news," I told her.

"Tell me the good news first."

"We get to sleep in next Sunday."

But word travels fast in Quaker circles and by that afternoon I'd been invited to speak at another meeting. It was a meeting with a reputation for theological rigidity and I wasn't anxious to be their pastor. So I preached a sermon whose theme was the sentence, "If you can't love homosexuals, you can't love God." I really didn't want to work there.

Afterwards, they went down to the basement to discuss whether to hire me. My wife and I sat upstairs, next to a heating grate, and listened. Things were going against me, until an elderly gentleman pointed out that I was young and would work for next to nothing, so the will of the Lord became clear to them and they hired me. I was at that church four years. By the time I left, I believed in hell.

I've often wondered why my first congregations resisted universalism to the degree they did. Initially, I attributed it to biblical fundamentalism, but have come to believe it is more complex than that. It was easy for me to believe in a gracious God, because I'd had gracious parents. It was easy for me to believe in a generous God, because I had always been generously treated. It was easy for me to believe in an afterlife of overflowing goodness and deep joy, for my present life had been filled with goodness and joy. Conversely, I find it difficult to believe in unrelenting evil, because the evil I've known has been transitory. I find it difficult to believe in an impatient God who gives up on some people, because I have been treated with patience and forbearance.

But the people in my first meetings had not been so blessed. Their daily lives were marked by scarcity, not plenty. Many of their family lives were marked by discord, not harmony.

I wasn't a Universalist because I was smarter than they. I wasn't a Universalist because I was more spiritual than they. I was a Universalist because I had been given a glimpse of God's love, and because of my fortunate life found it easy to believe the universe was ultimately benevolent. Had my life been filled with brokenness, need, and pain, I would have found the idea of grace unbelievable.

Of course, one thing that makes the idea of divine grace so incredible for so many is that those who claim to speak for God have been anything but gracious. I remember years and years ago, a man sitting on the front row taking careful notes while I was preaching. I was very flattered and when I learned he taught Sunday school, I made it a point to go to his class the next Sunday. So the next Sunday I arrived at meeting in time for Sunday school, went to his class, and listened as he began the class, saying, "So-called ministers of the gospel will tell you this . . ." then read my sermon line for line. That went on four years. As I got to know him, I learned two things about him. His early life had been horrendous, just filled with meanness. And the only way he felt able to save himself was to commit himself to a God as stern and intolerant as his parents.

I would talk to him about God's love, and he would immediately speak of God's justice. But it was an odd justice, condemning people who weren't sufficiently Christian, sending people to hell who'd never heard of Jesus.

How just is that? But it fit the man's experience, you see. He'd spent fifty-five years having those experiences confirmed, so there was no way I was going to be able to undo it in four years. Short of a peak experience, of course. Short of some transcendent moment that swung the needle of his spiritual compass toward grace.

Eventually, I would write a book about universalism called *If Grace Is True*. Prior to its release, the *Indianapolis Star* wrote an article about it, prompting fundamentalist Quakers in our yearly meeting to demand that my pastoral credentials be revoked. We call it a recording. They wanted my recording to be rescinded. Every year, for eight years, when we met for our annual business meeting, I was urged to recant what I had said in the book, and failing that, that my pastoral credentials be rescinded. And these people were Quakers, a denomination known for its religious tolerance.

I also received death threats, copies of the book burnt and charred, and predictions of my earthly demise. My sons became targeted for conversion by our town's mega-church and I was placed on their prayer list. Their pastor held up the book during a sermon and accused me of being an east coast liberal, though I had lived in Indiana all my life, most of it in the same small town. The church where I first became a Quaker wrote a letter demanding I be removed from the Quaker community, and when I wasn't, they withdrew.

People I had known my entire life would no longer speak to me. For eight years, the only church in our town that would have anything to do with me were the Unitarian Universalists, who, despite not identifying themselves as Christian, acted more like Christ than anyone else. Fortunately, my own church, located in the next town over, was very supportive.

After eight years of heresy trials, the matter was finally resolved when six fundamentalist congregations left our yearly meeting, and with them went the passion to see me punished. They are now in another yearly meeting, devoting their considerable power to punishing a Quaker meeting that had the temerity to welcome gays and lesbians.

It is all of the same thread. The same mindset that excluded blacks, that diminished women, that now rejects gays and lesbians, will also, in nearly every instance, reject grace. To them, grace is bad news, a slipping of truth, a letting down the guard. It is not to be celebrated, but feared. I have lived in their graceless worlds, where the rays of love seldom warm the land, where shadows prevail, where glee is found in retribution and payback. I have sat in churches where light never dawns, where laughter and joy are scorned, where the God of the Misers reigns on high.

I have seen love divided down to nothing, so that none was left to share with others. Clarence Jordan knew those places, too, but was led out of them, and then had the grace and courage to lead others out of them. The red hills of his Koinonia farm, which eventually held him in death, became for so many others our place of birth. His "Y'all come," opened to us the doorway to life, so we walked in, and there joined others at God's gracious feast. For living the Way, and for showing the Way to us, we gather to commend and commemorate his splendid life.

5

Who Would Jesus Bomb?

Ronnie McBrayer

William McBrayer, my seventh great-grandfather, came to the Lancaster Valley of Pennsylvania a generation before the American Revolutionary War. He was like so many of the Ulster-Scots who sailed to the new world during that period. Uprooted from Scotland a hundred years earlier to colonize Northern Ireland at the bequest of King James, and surviving conflict with the Irish, religious persecution, communal violence, and bouts of famine, the McBrayers found the Ulster Plantations to be less than ideal. So much so, that William desperately sold everything he had, took his Irish bride who was great with child, and boarded a ship for the unknown of the Americas. Upon arriving, he and his descendants dug deep into the rocky soil of Appalachia. Down the spine of those ancient mountains they came to Pennsylvania, the Virginias, the Carolinas, and for my direct ancestors, ultimately the hills of North Georgia where we remain ensconced to this very day.

It was Martin McBrayer who first came to Georgia, having acquired lot #142 in the Georgia Land Lottery of the 1830s; a large, bountiful piece of land on the Coosawatee River. He immediately left Buncombe County, North Carolina, loaded up his family and his slaves, and went forth to dispossess the indigenous Cherokee people off the land that had sustained them since primeval times. I must painfully admit that my ancestors contributed prominently to this travesty and tragedy of American history.

Meanwhile, my maternal ancestors were busy in Southern Appalachia as well, but a little thing called love complicated matters. John Jackson Welch Jr., my fourth great-grandfather fell in love with a North Carolinian Cherokee squaw named Sarah Wattee Brown. And though he had to bear the scorn of other colonizers, he married Sarah and followed the Cherokee custom of taking his wife's name. The chiefs renamed Welch *Wodigi Asgoli*, literally meaning "Brown Head" or "Head of the Brown Family." So the table was then set for my genetic history—a history shared by legions of families in the mountains of the Southeast: the combination of Ulster-Scot and Cherokee bloodlines, and the conflicting emotions that this heritage produces.

At once I am proud of my paternal family's name, tenacity, and courage to come so far and to do so much. I am also mortified over their use of force, injustice, and cruelty in taking what was not theirs. Equally, I am proud of my Cherokee history, though native blood is miniscule in my own veins. I wish had paid closer attention to my great-grandmother when she would say the Lord's Prayer in the native Cherokee language or when she removed a skin wart or some other blemish by reciting an old incantation passed on to her by the shamans. I mourn the loss of so much of that heritage. So yes, I am conflicted. But I'm not alone.

This conflict of allegiances, being pulled by love for one or other, is the default condition of Jesus followers living in the context of a nationalistic, militaristic, patriotic superpower. On one hand, our heritage and breeding instructs us to embrace our nation with abandon. On the other hand, we have this splinter in our brain that tells us that if we do that, we risk being untrue to the way of Jesus.

This is the premise of my presentation today, and the premise of my most recent book, from which these remarks are taken: *The Jesus Tribe: Following Christ in the Land of the Empire*.[1]

The way of Jesus and the American way are in conflict, no matter what is printed on this nation's coins or what hangs or does not hang on local court house walls. As much as we would like for there to be creatures known as "American Christians," no such animal exists. There are only Christians who happen to reside in America. This realization makes us feel odd, because it puts us at odds with the surrounding culture. We love

---

1. Ronnie McBrayer, *The Jesus Tribe: Following Christ in the Land of the Empire* (Macon GA: Smyth & Helwys, 2011).

America, but not at the expense of marginalizing the lordship of Jesus. We say the Pledge of Allegiance, but wish to do nothing that interferes with our supreme pledge as followers of Christ. And yes, we will sing the national anthem, but we will not ask Jesus to share his place of authority with the flag. In short, we must be more committed to Christ than to country. Our allegiance is to Jesus. He is our King. He is our Lord. It is his kingdom we serve. All other kingdoms and empires—including the United States—are in competition with the kingdom of God, and these cannot demand our principal loyalty.

Nowhere is this conflict more obvious than in Jesus' Sermon on the Mount. Matthew, it seems, collected these words of Jesus as the bedrock of our Lord's instruction. In fact, these may be the very words Matthew has in mind when at the conclusion of his Gospel he quotes Jesus saying, "Go and make disciples of all the nations, baptizing them in the name of the Father and the Son and the Holy Spirit. Teach these new disciples to obey *all the commands* I have given you" (Matthew 28:19–20). So, we might think of these three chapters in Matthew as Ben Witherington describes them: "Jesus' Greatest Hits."[2] These are a summary of what it means to be his disciple, a member of his tribe. These words serve as a means—maybe the most practical means—in actually following Jesus.

My youngest son, Braden is one of my best teachers, mainly because he is such a curious seeker. He is always investigating, exploring, and questioning things, especially so when it comes to things about Jesus. He came to me with one of his queries: "What is a Christian?" That's a good question, no doubt. I tried to shape an answer that a six-year-old could appreciate, so I said, "Braden, it's just like playing 'Follow the Leader.' A Christian is someone who follows Jesus." I was quite proud of my answer, but before I could get smug about it, the boy smirked back at me and said, "Well, I'm not going to be a Christian." Willing to take the bait, I asked him, "Why not?" He answered with his usual wisdom: "I'm not going to follow Jesus. I don't even know where he is going." Amen!

Yet, if we heed these words from the Sermon on the Mount, we do know where following Jesus will take us. It will lead us upstream and against the grain of the world around us; it will put us on a collision course with our culture, because the Sermon on the Mount teaches us that the most radical and world-changing thing we can do is "stop believing in the dominant systems and rules of this world," and live as "contradictions full of hope and

---

2. Ben Witherington III, *Matthew: Smyth & Helwys Bible Commentary* (Macon GA: Smyth & Helwys, 2006), 113.

promise."³ Our lives are our witness to the world, even though that witness will produce internal and external conflict. And why shouldn't conflict be inevitable? A non-conforming, transformed people will always smash up against the status quo.

This is where my colonizing and tribal heritage comes into union with Clarence Jordan. It's well established that Jesus' Sermon on the Mount was Clarence's favorite text, and anyone who spends time with Clarence sees this right way. And my own understanding of the Sermon on the Mount is directly informed by my exposure to the writings of Jordan. He rightly believed that the Sermon on the Mount was not a high and mighty ideal or a code of laws for some future utopia. It was not intended for debate or analysis; it was intended to be lived. These are concrete, real, workable solutions for living in this world as the followers of Jesus. As Clarence Jordan so simply said, "The Sermon on the Mount is not for the purpose of inspiration, but perspiration." The time for sermonizing must come to an end, and be replaced with living out what we have heard. So for Clarence, to refuse the words and ways of Jesus, here in the Sermon on the Mount and no matter how much conflicting angst these words produce, was to refuse Christianity itself—it was to refuse Christ.

That said, let me go straight to what has been for me the greatest conflict produced by the Sermon on the Mount. This conflict is unavoidable, but ironically, may be the best place for the church to recapture its Jesus-tuned voice in the twenty-first century, and the most profitable place to embrace the way of Jesus within our current society. This issue—this conflict—is conflict! It is Jesus' instructions regarding peace and nonviolence, one of the major, if not the major theme of the Sermon on the Mount. In all my decades of being in the church—from childhood to the pastorate, from family Bible studies to denominational leadership, from the primary Sunday school class to seminary—not once did I hear a thorough sermon, commentary, or Bible lesson that seriously took on the nonviolent words of Jesus. But how could I? It would require a conflict of conscience for most of us, if not outright cognitive dissonance to do so, as violence is absolutely required to maintain the security of an empire, and the church is usually very much at home in the empire.

Nowadays, as I write and speak on a wide variety of topics, this one subject—Jesus' way of nonviolence—always generates the most controversy, and blisteringly so. Why is this? It is because we believe a lie, and no

3. Karl Barth, *Church Dogmatics* (Edinburgh: T. and T. Clark, 1961), 4.3.2.

one likes to think that their belief system is erroneous. But we believe that violence can somehow save us; we believe that killing will prevent future killing; we believe that warfare will produce peace. We believe that stockpiles of weapons and ammunition will serve as a deterrent to war. We simply trust the way of the gun more than we trust the words and way of Jesus.

When confronted with this, well, it makes people angry. But I can't blame anyone for getting angry. I don't like it either—not one bit, because at the core of who I am, I am a violent, revenge-taking, retaliatory person. We all are! And I must admit that personally, I find this section of the Sermon on the Mount the most difficult to put into practice. I feel myself colliding with the dominant values around me, with parishioners, friends, and even family. (My internal conflict is heightened as I can make no guarantees that I would "turn the other cheek" if violence was brought against my person or family; I might respond with killing vengeance.) But we must do business with this man Jesus, and realize that either: 1) Jesus did not mean what he said, 2) He did not say what he meant, or 3) He actually said what he meant and meant what he said.

But if Jesus said what he meant and meant what he said about non-violence, it had to be regarded as irrational—back when he first said it—and even more so today. Today, a military invasion can be launched within minutes, a terrorist attack can be executed with a single combatant and with the push of a button, thousands can be turned to ash in a matter of seconds. We have never before held in our hands such awful destructive power, and we are convinced that if this power is used preemptively, efficiently, and "righteously" then Jesus' words can be dismissed as hopelessly unrealistic in this violent world. We are so convinced of this that the country in which we live is the greatest military power in the world—in history—and yet we claim to be the most Christian. How can these two things be compatible?

A bumper sticker I saw while sitting in traffic frames this inconsistency extremely well. It simply asked the question: "Who Would Jesus Bomb?" The answer from many card-carrying, pew-occupying, Bible-reading Christians who often lead the empire's march into battle and bloodshed is to bomb the hell out of anyone who threatens our national or personal security. Such violence does more than kill people. As followers of Jesus, this use of violence kills our faith.

Violence promises us something we all deeply desire, something we genuinely want; violence promises us peace. Violence promises us, that in the end, when the last battle is fought, the last bomb is dropped, and the last enemy is slain, we will have what we always dreamed of—safety, a world without suffering, death or bloodshed; a world at rest. Yet, these are the very things Christ offers with the Kingdom of God. A world where the lamb will lay down with the lion, where swords are beaten into plowshares, where mercy and justice flow down like the waters, where every tear will be wiped away from our eyes, and where there will be no more death or sorrow or crying or pain. Christ and violence seem to offer the same final result, the two being competitors for our allegiance. But if we resort to violence, even to combat violence, we have been lured away from the path of Christ. We are trusting war to save and redeem us instead of Jesus.

This enticement to redemptive violence is very real and one that Jesus experienced for himself. The prelude to the Sermon on the Mount is Jesus' baptism and wilderness temptations in Matthew 4, a prelude that deserves brief attention here. As Jesus' public ministry began, looming questions would have been hanging over him: "What kind of power will this Jesus use to accomplish his purposes and goals? What method will this man employ to bring his ambitions to bear on the world around him? What path will he take to the throne of the nation?" The answers to these questions begin to take shape as, still dripping wet from his baptism, Jesus is driven into the desert. And after spending forty days and nights fasting, like a landlord showing up at the most inopportune time to badger a tenant for the rent, the devil comes a calling with temptations of bread, skydives, and mountain climbing.

These temptations were not simple appeals to what the preachers of my childhood called the "flesh." They were more devilish than that. They were attempts to provide Jesus with an easier means at achieving his mission, to build an empire through systematic force and domination, rather than establishing the kingdom of God through the inverted power of love, justice, and suffering sacrifice. The devil invited Jesus to reach a sanctified finish by following an unsanctioned path. This path was paved with bread, temples, and mountains. Or put another way: economics, religion, and violence, the major structures upon which all empires are built; this is what Donald Kraybill calls the three-legged stool of human power.[4]

To the third temptation: The Tempter draws Jesus to a high mountain and then draws his attention to an area where Jesus' superhuman powers could do some real good—the kingdoms of the world. Someone with the right charisma, revolutionary strength, and idealism could unite the people of God and re-establish Israel's glory. What was needed was strong political

---

4. Donald B. Kraybill, *The Upside Down Kingdom*, 25th anniversary edition (Scottdale, PA: Herald, 2003), 33.

and military leadership. The Tempter laid this option squarely on the table for Jesus to take up as his own: "Re-institutionalize the nation and from there, exterminate all enemies, and bring peace to the world. Jesus, you could straighten this entire sordid affair out." Jesus answers this temptation as he answered all three: He will not employ the established human ways and systems of power for his own purposes, no matter how noble, because he knows that no human power can serve God's ultimate will.

See, the only way one can gain "the kingdoms of the world and all their glory" is to follow the Tempter's way of violence. To hold political power in the land of empire is to hold military power and to use it in defending and expanding national borders against internal and external enemies. If one is going to rule an empire or even maintain the security of a nation, one must be willing to wage war. War, in this context, is a requirement of nations, particularly a nation like America whose borders and interests stretch over so much land and sea. That is simply what nations must do, and anyone who thinks differently is not being practical.

To that end, you might remember that in December 2009, President Barack Obama delivered an historical speech at his acceptance of the Nobel Peace Prize in Oslo. For a speech about peace, his words acknowledged an absolute necessity to wage war. With words that could have been spoken by any United States President he said: "As a head of state sworn to protect and defend my nation . . . I face the world as it is, and cannot stand idle in the face of threats to the American people . . . To say that force is sometimes necessary is not a call to cynicism—it is a recognition of history, the imperfections of man and the limits of reason. So yes, the instruments of war do have a role to play in preserving the peace."[5]

Speaking as one responsible for the empire, Barack Obama's words were exactly on target. America will fight against her enemies with bombs, soldiers, and priceless, sacrificial blood to protect the American way of life and preserve the nation. But I do not believe the church should employ or sanction these methods. Violence might be necessary in the world of empire, but if Jesus teaches us anything, he teaches us that what the world presumes as necessary, in his view and in his way may not be necessary at all.

---

5 Barack H. Obama, "Remarks by the President at the Acceptance of the Nobel Peace Prize," delivered at Oslo City Hall, Oslo, Norway, December 10, 2009. Available online at <http://www.whitehouse.gov/the-pressoffice/remarks-president-acceptance-nobel-peace-prize>.

Jesus gives us practical examples to this effect. There are three such examples in the Sermon on the Mount: Being slapped, being forced to walk a long distance, and being dragged into court. All three have a common denominator. All of these are examples of injustice inflicted upon the follower of Jesus. Beginning with the slap to the cheek, there is a subtle but important word in Jesus' command that his original hearers would have understood well. It is the word, "right." If someone slaps you on the "right" cheek, offer the other one also. Being struck on the right cheek was a description of someone getting backhanded. A strike on the right cheek was an act intended to humiliate, used by a person in power over someone who was powerless or vulnerable. It was how a master would treat a slave, a landowner would treat a sharecropper, a Roman soldier would treat a Jewish citizen, a husband would treat a wife in that chauvinistic culture.

Jesus proposes neither an act of retaliation, nor does he advocate a humiliated cowering on the ground in submission. He offers a third way: turn the other cheek. Rob the aggressor of his power to humiliate. By offering the other cheek the disciple says to his or her antagonist, "I refuse to be humiliated. Try again." It is nonviolent, dignified resistance that exposes the act as wrong, and turns the humiliation back on the perpetuator of violence.

Another example: If you are being unjustly treated in the court systems—someone is taking your shirt and essentially taking your dignity—then give them your coat. Imagine what would happen if at the height of the legal deliberations the victim stood up, publicly stripped naked before the prosecutor and judge and said, "You might as well have it all," and walked out. It would shame the system that allows such injustice to prevail. And a third scenario: A soldier forcing someone to carry his load. In Jesus' day a Roman soldier could come along and demand a person to carry his backpack for up to a mile, no questions asked. A farmer busy on his farm or a shopkeeper in her shop or a baker at the oven; a soldier picks one of these people out of the crowd to become his personal donkey, and the individual had to comply or face the violent consequences. The good news is the compulsion was only enforceable for a mile. To this Jesus says, "Go two miles." Why? It robbed the soldier of his power and actually put his neck in the noose. Should the commanding officer arrive halfway through that second mile, how is the two-mile journey going to be explained? Further, the disciple was nonviolently showing that he would not be manipulated or controlled by abusive power.

In each and every case, Jesus' instruction in response to violence is the same: Do not lash out in retaliation, but do not cower in fearful compliance. Trump the power of the world with the upside down power of the kingdom of God. They may slap you. They may take everything you own. They may walk you to the moon and back, but do not lash out, and do not let up. This is what it means to turn the other cheek and love our enemy.

Here is a tribal example of what this looks like today. Following the American Civil War, the United States Army moved in force into the western reaches of the continent. One by one native people groups were exterminated, forcibly moved on to reservations, or starved into submission. Portions of the Lakota Sioux nation, however, led by men like Red Cloud and Sitting Bull, waged war with the empire. This war came to a cataclysmic end in 1876 at the Battle of the Little Bighorn. This was the literal end of most of the Seventh Calvary led by George A. Custer, as they were soundly defeated. But it was also the end of the Lakota Sioux's fight for independence, as in the aftermath American public opinion about "the Indian problem" galvanized and all western tribes were subjugated.

A year after the Battle of the Little Bighorn, with gold discovered in the Black Hills of the Dakotas, the United States government broke its treaty with the Lakota Sioux and demanded these sacred lands. The tribe refused, so the land was stolen. One hundred and three years later, in 1980, the Supreme Court ordered the federal government to pay $105 million to eight Lakota Sioux tribes for the land that had been taken from them. This was the original value attached to the land plus a century of interest. It was a landmark decision, but the Lakota Sioux refused this pay-off. As of today, the trust fund set aside by the courts is almost one billion dollars.

Why did the tribal councils refuse this payment? It is because the Lakota Sioux consider the Black Hills sacred ground to which no dollar amount can be attached. Further, to take the money would be to bless the theft. The only solution offered officially from the Lakota Sioux nation is the trust fund payment and the return of the land. The tribe is willing to wait—turning the other cheek—out of principle and justice, even while a billion dollars sits in the bank, dollars that would feed many hungry mouths and shelter many families. This is a huge example of how this kind of approach can work itself out in a hundred different ways.

It should go without saying that the nonviolent teachings of Jesus will never be accepted by the empire around us. From a practical standpoint, they shouldn't be. A person, people, or nation must fight to stay alive in the world in which we live. If you find this pragmatism to be too outrageous, it is simply a misunderstanding of unredeemed human nature. From angry little boys on the playground to heads of state with their fingers on the firing button, it is natural to want to prevail over your enemy, even kill them if you must. Violence is necessary to stay alive and is a natural part of being human. Those who think that talk or dialogue alone can end all conflict in the world have a fatalistically flawed, utopian view of how things really are.

But to follow Christ is to be set free from human nature, to let go of what the world deems necessary for survival. To follow Christ means we have found a new way to live, a new way to be human, and that we are not fastened to what we once were. The old has gone, and the new has come. As Christians we must oppose and resist violence of all kinds, because violence is a tool of the fallen, unredeemed nature. It is of the world, and does not reflect the good and gracious nature of our Father. The role of the Jesus Tribe is to be aliens and strangers, to be a counter-culture that goes against the flow of what is otherwise accepted, so Jesus followers refuse violence, even when such violence appears to be for honorable ends.

Thus, this way of Jesus cannot be characterized as traditional pacifism. Traditional pacifism is a wonderful ideal, but there is no power within it to actually accomplish peace. Traditional pacifism ignores—and this is supremely important—the theological and Christological motivation and power for peace. "You will be acting as true children of your Father in heaven" (Matt 5:45), Jesus says. We follow Jesus' way of nonviolence because this is how God treats his enemies. Graciousness toward others—even those who want to kill us—is like God: "You are to be perfect, even as your Father in heaven is perfect" (Matt 5:48).

The Greek word for "perfect" in the Sermon on the Mount is a form of *teleos*. It was a word used to describe the appropriate sacrificial lamb that was without defect. It described a graduating student who had completed his course of study and was now ready to face the task for which he had been trained. And the word was used to describe a child or adolescent who had grown past immaturity to the place of adulthood. *Teleos* is not functional or positional perfection. It is the realization of one's vocation and the gaining of maturity. William Barclay said, "A man is perfect (*teleos*) if he realizes the purpose for which he was created and sent into the world."[6]

As followers within the Jesus Tribe, our purpose is to reflect the wholeness and identity of our Father in heaven. We are to be grace-filled manifestations of who he is as his Son shines through us. God is made

---

6. William Barclay, *The Gospel of Matthew*, vol. 1, rev. ed. (Philadelphia: Westminster, 1975), 177.

visible and tangible, not with our declarations of truth or reciting of the creeds, but God is made visible in us and in our world, when we respond to others as he responds to them. And how does God respond to people? With grace and goodness as he sends "his sunlight to both the evil and the good, and he sends rain on the just and the unjust alike." God's love simply knows no limit: Suicide bombers, serial killers, thieves, prostitutes, Wall Street pirates, dirty politicians, exploiters of the innocent. He doesn't approve of these injustices, but still he loves those in his world. "While we were still sinners, Christ died for us," and while we were God's enemies he took the necessary loving steps to reconcile us to himself.

So we love, not because it will work, or because it is practical, or because it will "change the world." We love because it is how God treats the world, and this love does much more than make us "act differently." It actually makes us different as Christ lives his life through us. Love is how we live and act. Love is how we operate. Granted, such love may appear powerless in the face of violence, and violence may eventually be used against those who won't play by the rules, but violence and death are not the end of the follower of Jesus. "Crucifixions have a way of being followed by resurrections," Clarence said, and resurrections cannot be defeated.

So how do we put this peaceful, nonviolent way of Jesus into practice? Glen Stassen and David Gushee have added a useful word to my vocabulary. It is the word "performative." The kingdom of God is "performative," they say. They explain: "What God is doing in the world is his performance, but we are invited to actively participate. As we participate we become what God desires for his world."[7] God's performance and our participation: This takes the pressure off of the disciple, making our biggest responsibility one of surrender. If we give up on our own abilities to bring the Kingdom of God into the world, if we loosen our grip on what we want and what we think we can do, then that space will be filled by what God can do. Nonviolence and peace-making is God's love working through us, not what we do on our own, and God knows God will have to do it for us if it is going to get done. We have to rely upon him to live any portion of the Christian life, especially as it relates to turning the other cheek, walking the second mile, and loving our enemies.

A final metaphor from my Cherokee heritage is appropriate as we conclude: What brought my McBrayer ancestors to Georgia almost 200

---

7. Glen H. Stassen and David P. Gushee, *Kingdom Ethics; Following Jesus in Contemporary Context* (Downers Grove, IL: Intervarsity, 2003), 21.

years ago was the discovery a few shiny rocks in a mountain stream, just a few rolling hills away from my childhood home. It was gold, and whatever tenuous hold the Cherokee had on their ancestral home was now broken. Greedy prospectors came pouring over the hills with picks, shovels, dreams of wealth, and a new Georgia folk song on their lips: "All I ask in this creation is a pretty little wife and big plantation, way up yonder in the Cherokee Nation." So it was that a decade after gold was discovered in "them thar hills," the United States Army and the Georgia Militia began assembling the remaining Cherokee for the thousand mile forced march across the Mississippi River to what is now the state of Oklahoma.

"Build a fire under them," Andrew Jackson had instructed a Georgia congressman. "When it gets hot enough, they'll move." And the empire's fire burned hot as any hell: farms were stolen; homes were burned; violence was normalized; Christian missionaries living among the Cherokee were forced to take oaths of allegiance to the state of Georgia or be imprisoned (and some were). And once assembled, hundreds of Cherokee died in the stockades, held as they were, like caged animals for months. Those deaths were just the start; of the 16,000 Cherokee put on the Trail of Tears, more than a quarter died of starvation, exposure, and disease.

By the time of the Trail of Tears many of the Cherokee had become followers of Jesus. "Jesus has risen from the dead. Only the greatest shaman could do that," some of their chiefs proclaimed. So in spite of the fact that many Christians had been instrumental in their sufferings, they placed their faith in Christ and called upon that faith as they marched across the continent, asking Jesus to help them. Alongside their traditional songs and chants, the Cherokee lifted their spirits by singing the frontier hymns of the faith. One such hymn, "Guide Me, Oh Jehovah," was lifted as a prayer for the journey. I offer it here as the same, and it is my hope that we in the Jesus Tribe will sing this as a prayer of dependence on our journey through the land of the Empire:

> Guide me, Oh Jehovah, on this path here below.
> You are very strong and I am very weak.
> All the time, all the time; help me, all the time.
>
> Amen.

6

Standing in the Gap

Dolphus Weary

What a joy it's been for my wife, Rosie, and me to be here for the Clarence Jordan Symposium. We've been taken from emotional highs to emotional lows. There were times when Rosie had to reach over and pass me some tissues. But that's OK. Because it's important for us to understand the passion, the pain that we've come from so we can better know where to go in the future.

Let me share my Koinonia/Habitat story. I served on the board of Koinonia Farm for a number of years, but my Koinonia story is this: I was on the board when Millard Fuller was there as executive director of Koinonia. He brought to the board the idea of taking the Fund for Humanity and making it a nationwide house building program. And we, the board, turned him down. We, the board, decided not to do it, and Millard left Koinonia a year later and formed Habitat for Humanity. And now Habitat is known all over the world.

Koinonia? Significant. Habitat for Humanity? Significant. All of God's works are significant.

I want to look at a passage of Scripture, Exodus, chapter thirty-two. We're going to talk about what it means to stand in the gap. Now, the people began to question God. The people saw Moses delayed coming down from the mountain, the people gathered together to Aaron and said, "Come, make us gods that we can go before." And Aaron said, "Bring me all your gold." And the people took off their gold earrings, melted them down and created another god.

Then the Lord said to Moses, "Go down! *Your* people, whom *you* brought out of the land of Egypt, have corrupted themselves!" That's God talking to Moses. *Your* people. *You* brought them out. "They have turned aside quickly and gone a different way. I have seen this people and they are indeed a stiff-necked people." I wonder if Christians are a stiff-necked people. As soon as we get a dime above a nickel, we start looking down our noses at other people. As soon as we learn one or two Bible verses, we start looking down our noses at people who are still struggling. How quickly we forget from where God has brought us.

Then God told Moses to leave him alone, "that my wrath might burn hot against them and I might consume them." Moses, they're ungrateful! Moses, they're unfaithful! Now this is how he lays it out: Moses had two choices. The first choice he had was, "Ok, God, I'm joining you!" Ego could have taken over Moses' heart. "That's a good idea, God. Let's get rid of them and start over with me." But here's the good news, the second choice: Moses stood in the gap. He dared to stand in the gap between a stiff-necked people and a holy God.

Moses said, "Remember your promise to your servant, to Abraham and to Isaac and to Jacob." He reminds God of that. "So the Lord relented from the harm which he had thought in his heart." In the Living Bible it says that "the Lord changed his mind and spared them."

What a choice. We have choices all the time. Are we going to live a selfish, individualistic life? In America we learn how to be selfish and individualistic. Please hear this: we *learn* how to be selfish and individualistic. We learn how to think "me first" and we've got a me-first gospel and a me-first Christianity.

We've got to learn how to say, "Thank you, God, for standing in the gap for me!" Because when Jesus hung on the cross at Calvary, he stood in the gap for every single one of us. It meant that every single one of us has access to the King of Kings and the Lord of Lords, because he stood in the gap on the cross on our behalf. And when he said it was finished, it didn't mean for just the white folk, or for just the black folk. John 3:16 says that *whosoever* believes, and in Dolphus Weary's definition of "whosoever," well, it's just any ol' body.

Who's going to stand in the gap and take that message to everybody? Well, let me just remind you that Clarence Jordan stood in the gap. For many years he stood in the gap; for many years he suffered and those who joined him suffered. But they stood in the gap anyhow! We can look back in history at all the terrible and deadly stuff, but we're not to stay there. We're supposed to learn from it so we can move forward and *we* can stand in the gap for others. That's the reason why we have to look back.

I'm always telling black folk not to look back too long, because if you look back too long you can end up being angry and bitter. Don't look back too long, but look back long enough to see from where God has brought us. Now let's look at where God wants to take us.

I get sick and tired of talking to people who are always talking about "one day." You know the stories. There is not a single church in Sumter County that doesn't believe in unity in the body of Christ. The problem is not believing, the problem is doing. I talk to people all the time who say, "We ought to love our neighbor—all of us." When do we stop talking about "ought" and start talking about what we're doing in order to get there?

Millard Fuller stood in the gap. Housing for poor around the world. The Fuller Center is standing in the gap, Habitat for Humanity is standing in the gap. Who are you standing in the gap for? I trust you're standing in the gap for your children and your grandchildren. And please, don't give up on them. You know why? You're not God. I don't know what you're going through, or what your children or your grandchildren are going through, but I know you don't have the luxury of giving up, because you're not God. You don't know what tomorrow will bring. You might want to give up on somebody, but you don't know what tomorrow will bring. God never called for you to change anybody. You were never called to change your spouse. Now don't be kicking anybody under the table . . . God did not call you to change your spouse. If it's in your job description, leave this service, go home, get your computer, and hit the delete button.

But here's the good news: he did call for you to model out, to show an example. That's what he called for us to do. That's the struggle we have in society, that's the struggle we have in politics, because we think it's our job to change the person we're talking to, rather than listen to the person we're with.

I was preaching at a 3,000-member church out in California and this woman came up to me and said, "I appreciate your message, but listen to this: I disagree with you because I don't see how anybody can be a Christian and be a Democrat." And I went, "OK, I have to preach another service, so I don't have time to talk to you right now, but I'm pretty sure in this church of 3,000 there must be somebody who's a Christian and a Democrat. Why don't you take them out to lunch or dinner and spend time with them to learn why they are a Christian and a Democrat?" And she said, "I tried that and they didn't listen."

Therein is the problem. We don't talk to people to learn from them, we talk to people to change them. We need to spend more time talking to people to learn, praying for them, and less time trying to change them.

Your fellow church members—stand in the gap for them. Your neighbors—stand in the gap for them. And who's going to stand in the gap for those people you don't like? Moses stood in the gap for the children of Israel, and God wants us to stand in the gap for others.

My wife and I have chosen to trust God to use us to stand in the gap for the poor and oppressed in rural Mississippi. We grew up there and became Christians through the ministry of John Perkins in Mendenhall, Mississippi. I played basketball in high school and one of my dreams was how to escape from Mississippi. I finally got a basketball scholarship to go to school in California, boarded the bus in Jackson and the only thing I thought about was, "Lord, I'm leaving Mississippi and I ain't never coming back."

I was playing basketball in the Philippines on a Christian basketball team over there and the coach said to me, "Dolphus, why not consider becoming a missionary overseas?" And the first thing out of my mouth was, "Anyplace but Mississippi!"

The Holy Spirit began to deal with my heart. "Dolphus, are you thinking about going to a mission field, or are you running away from a mission field?" Believers, there are mission fields all around us that we choose to run away from. So then God brought us back to Mississippi. We moved back in 1971, chasing another dream, which was, "How can we make this gospel available to the poor community?" And over a twenty-seven-year history, we built a ministry that had a health clinic, an elementary school, a thrift store, a farm, a law office, a housing ministry, a recreation ministry, and an adult education ministry that became a model ministry dealing with the poor in Mendenhall.

We left that ministry in 1998 and God moved us to a new ministry called Mission Ministry. And now we're standing in the gap between black Christians and white Christians and saying it's time for us to learn to love each other, because we all call ourselves Christians. Let's get the Christians to do what Christians are supposed to do and let the heathens learn from us.

Sometimes we expect Jesus to do stuff we won't do. But we need to model it out. And sometimes we get tired standing in the gap between black Christians and white Christians, but it's important that someone keep bringing people back to reality. The reality is that in Christ Jesus, we are part of a new family.

I have the privilege of preaching in churches across the state, preaching across racial and denominational lines, and it's always the same message. If it's in a black church, it's, "You need to learn to become a child of God first, and black second." I hear all this noise, "What are we gonna do about all the Mexicans coming?" The church ought to be saying, "Let them come." Politicians might say something different, but the church ought to be saying, "Let them come!" We let them come and we lead them to Jesus and then maybe they'll go to Mexico as missionaries.

The church, standing in the gap, ought to have a different voice than the world.

7

Cotton Patch Reconciliation

Transforming Historical Harms

DAVID ANDERSON HOOKER

While I am long familiar with Koinonia and its place in the struggle for human dignity and equality in the Southern U.S., I would not by any stretch consider myself a Clarence Jordan scholar. I will say that this symposium presented me with an incredible opportunity to learn more about him as a person, his life and his work. But as I considered the basis of my remarks, I realized that those who invited me to present also knew that I was not a Jordan scholar and they asked me to present anyway, which tells me that they wanted me to talk about something I have a deeper familiarity with, which, in this case, is grassroots peace-building, and then connect that to the life and work of Clarence Jordan. So that is my intention.

I want to talk for a few minutes about the idea of transforming historical harms and then relate the ideas and practices to Clarence's Cotton Patch Gospels, to demonstrate their significance and continuing relevance. In the same way that I consider other versions of Scripture to be living documents I recognize that the Cotton Patch Gospels also have a continuing significance. While I will reference the Gospels, I am primarily interested in talking about what allows trauma and conflict to persist and to be passed on for several generations even when the original causes or circumstances that produced the trauma are no longer present.

My remarks are grounded in thirty years of experience in conflict transformation, post-riot reconciliation practices, and racial dialogue, and more explicitly in three aspects of my more recent work. First, since shortly after September 11, 2001, I have been involved in training religious, government, and civic leaders, and front line caregivers in ideas of trauma, trauma healing, and self-care. Secondly, for the past five years, I served as the director of research and training for a group called Coming to the Table (comingtothetable.org). This started as a project to link a group of descendants of the formerly enslaved with descendants of former enslavers, in a dialogue and healing process. The audience, circle of participants, and focus expanded significantly to consider other activities and interested parties who wanted to also consider other approaches to racial healing in the United States. While doing the work of developing engagement models for folks from the U.S., I also studied reconciliation efforts between European descendants and first nation's folks in Australia, Canada, and New Zealand as well as reconciliation efforts in Cambodia. My third set of experiences was varied levels of involvement with peace-building for communities when their governments were in transition after years of civil war or brutal violence, such as in Bosnia, Southern Sudan, Sierra Leone, and Liberia.

I've learned several key factors from all these experiences. Healing is hard but possible. No matter how long people have experienced harm or been burdened with the results of traumagenic experiences, there is an ever present energy that supports healing. The longer unhealed trauma goes unaddressed the more deeply it is entrenched in the everyday experiences of people, to the point where it is normalized and made invisible. Shifts in both narrative and performative communication are required to move towards peace and community. The gospel of Jesus and the version known as the Cotton Patch Gospels present us with fine examples of how both narrative and performative can be shifted towards justice and peace.

In order to connect the Cotton Patch writings to the practices of grassroots peace-building, I propose to talk in three sections. First, there will be a very brief discussion of trauma, the creation of traumagenic societies, and mechanisms that support the multigenerational transmission of trauma sources, thought, and behavior. The *mechanisms* are really important because they point to an approach to transforming historical harms.

Second, I will describe the principles and practices that we have identified as being essential to peace-building in the face of multigenerational trauma. Finally, I want to talk about the role of narrative, discourse, and the Gospels in building peace.

To set the stage for this conversation and in order to make it very practical for us, I'd like each of you to think about a multigenerational trauma or multigenerational conflict that you are either directly involved in or that is of interest to you. As I talk about the mechanisms and possible responses, think in terms of the specific trauma you've identified, so our questions can be focused.

Trauma

A great resource for those interested in learning more about trauma is Peter Levine's *Waking the Tiger*.[1] What Levine helps us think about is that there is not a specific event or situation that is itself traumatic. What Levine says is that *trauma is the response to a circumstance that overwhelms the capacity to respond*. This is helpful because it points out that in any given circumstance individuals will respond differently. Not every circumstance is equally overwhelming to everyone who has the experience *and* not everyone who is equally overwhelmed will respond the same way. Trauma impacts physically, mentally or emotionally, behaviorally, and spiritually. Trauma can have both negative and positive responses. As a result of being overwhelmed, someone might question his or her faith while another person in response to the same circumstance might have an increased or deepened faith. It is also the case that entire communities and societies could experience an event that overwhelms the community's collective capacity to respond. The responses to this circumstance would be described as *collective or community trauma*.

Trauma responses might be short lived and in other instances they could be long term. In the case of personal trauma, the types of responses we are most familiar with fit into the complex of behaviors that is often classified as PTSD—Post Traumatic Stress Disorder. There are a variety of clinical interventions and other "treatments" for PTSD and other forms of long term individual trauma responses. What is more our focus now is the fact that in the same way that trauma responses in individuals can be long

---

1. Peter Levine and Ann Frederick, *Waking the Tiger: Healing Trauma* (Berkeley, CA: North Atlantic Books, 1997).

term, communities can also have long term trauma responses. Often these trauma responses get institutionalized by various policies, practices, rituals, and institutional structures. Long term responses in communities are what I call traumagenic societies. This is because the genesis of the trauma is no longer the original event but rather the patterns, practices, beliefs, and institutions of the society that produce and reproduce the trauma.

A traumageneic society is one in which the society has incorporated (de facto or de jure) policies, practices, and beliefs that continue to traumatize specific groups within the society to that group's detriment and the benefit of others. Over an extended period, the traumageneic society reflects the continuing trauma through clear disparities in health, welfare, economics, and many other forms of mental, emotional, physical, and spiritual well-being. Over time, the group feature (race, ethnicity, religion, etc.) that was the basis of the original traumageneic policies, practices, and beliefs becomes a clear predictor of "dysfunction" or lack of well-being.

Nicaraguan psychologist Martha Cabrera also describes societies that have become traumageneic; her term for them is "multiply wounded societies." "When one has a lot of accumulated pain, one loses the capacity to communicate with others. The ability to communicate, to be flexible and tolerant is enormously reduced among people who have a number of unresolved personal traumas. The characteristics vital to a person's ability to function adequately become affected. The loss of solidarity that we lament in today's [society] has to do with loss of trust between people . . . [T]he strengthening of an institution is based on mutual trust and that is one of the things that's lost when there is an accumulation of pain and misplaced intolerance and inflexibility."[2]

A whole society can be impacted from trauma and pass it on because trauma impacts victims, witnesses, and perpetrators. The following is excerpt from the Virginia Constitutional Convention, July 1773, by George Masson, a slaveholder and founding father of the United States. He identifies ways that whole groups of offenders can pass dehumanizing behavior on to the next generation. "Slavery . . . That slow poison, which is daily contaminating the minds and morals of our people. Every gentlemen here is born a petty tyrant. Practiced in the arts of despotism and cruelty, we become callous to the dictates of Humanity and all the finer feelings of the soul. Taught to regard our own species in the most object and contemptible

---

2. Martha Cabrera, "Living and Surviving in a Multiply Wounded Country." www.medico.de/download/report26/ps_cabrera_en.pdf.

degree below us, we lose the idea of the dignity of Man, which the hand of nature had implanted in us, for great and useful purposes."

When the wounding is not addressed, victims, witnesses, and perpetrators remain in cycles of victimhood and violence/aggression/domination. Those who are aggressors often see the only other option to dominating others as being dominated, so they work hard to maintain their positions. Those who are victims of harm struggle to find a sense of agency and break out of the cycle. Over time, the aggression and justification can become part of culture and institutions, no longer relying only on individuals and individual experience to promote the cycles and pass them on to the next generation.

Mechanisms for the Perpetuation of Trauma

There are two principles that perpetuate trauma and make peace less possible.[3]

The "legacy" and "aftermath" of historical trauma act as invisible and unconscious limits upon individual and/or collective capacity of the historically traumatized community's capacity to exercise power and agency in seeking self-definition and self-determination. These same legacies and aftermaths also constrain the humanity and empathetic expression of individuals and groups who are burdened with a historically privileged station and entitlement mentality and effects of policies and practices that systemically disenfranchise others.

Legacy: "Legacy" is the collection of beliefs, ideas, myths, prejudices and biases that are disseminated and then inherited by and/or about differing groups. Often, today's legacy was the original basis/justification for disparate treatment of one group by another. Legacies establish notions of superiority and inferiority or confirm the character of a marginalized group. Legacy is often built into the official "history," the folklore and language of a people in ways that subtly and blatantly pass on the bias and justify societal arrangements such as oppression, repression, enslavement, isolation, or even genocide or cultural extinction.

Aftermath: When you think of "aftermath" the general picture that often comes to mind is the debris, rubble, or structural remains of a natural disaster or war. The torn down buildings, the broken levees, and the

---

3. The following section draws from David Anderson Hooker and Amy Potter Czjaikowski, "Transforming Historical Harms," Eastern Mennonite University, 2012.

bomb craters are all examples of "aftermath—the broken and tattered infrastructure and material that remains after a society has experienced great destruction." This is the imagery that best depicts a society after a group-based historical trauma such as the Transatlantic Slave Trade. After the earthquake, the rubble from the building still remains and has to go somewhere. Usually in efforts to rebuild the society, rubble is simply buried or pulverized but the building blocks and materials are still very present in the environment.

This is the case for the "aftermath" of historic trauma as well. In relationship to multigenerational trauma, "aftermath" refers to the institutions, laws, political and economic structures, as well as the official story conveyed and enforced by a society's supporting systems (education, religion, social service, criminal justice, etc.), which were formed to enforce or reinforce particular aspects of a legacy. This aftermath remains long after the overt traumageneic policies and practices have been stopped or reconsidered. Unless there is a conscious and extended effort to unveil the legacy and connect it to the aftermath, the aftermath is usually still present even when the legacy (i.e., myths, prejudices, and biases) has been officially discredited! Also, because "aftermath" is built into structures, rules, traditions, and practices, there is no personal action or even intention required to maintain the designed and desired power-wounding and marginalizing effects.

Legacy and aftermath cooperate in this way to perpetuate a massive trauma: individuals and groups have experiences of trauma (victim, perpetrator or witness); they build systems, implement laws and policies and define their relationships with other people based on values and beliefs that they hold. Many of the values that they hold were consciously or unconsciously formed as justification for or in response to traumagenic behavior. The systems and other political and social arrangements are, thereby, founded in and based on trauma causing and trauma effected beliefs. Even when the attitudes and even values (legacy) shift, the systems, laws, and relational patterns are much slower to shift and therefore maintain the trauma causing/trauma reactive patterns in society. The trauma is transferred without intention or attention. In attempting to undo or mitigate the effects of both the legacy and aftermath, there has to be significant attention paid to both the hidden discourse and also the systems that it gives rise. They both must be addressed at the same time.

These values play a significant role in determining the dimensions of the Transforming Historical Harms Model, including history, healing, connection, and action.

The framework that we developed to begin to transform historical harms incorporates the four values listed above and identifies four areas of activity that people can engage in: exploring approaches to facing history that help identify ways to move forward; learning how connection—building relationships across historical divisions—can create partnerships capable of working towards effective change; identifying the importance of creating spaces that welcome healing (of mind, body and spirit) from past injustices and methods that support both individual and collective healing; and taking action to address beliefs, behaviors, and structures responsible for ongoing harms.

Another vital insight from the Transforming Historical Harms Model is the power of narrative. Values of society are carried in stories and shared from generation to generation by the stories we tell and the stories we live into. Stories are told to explain/justify rituals and institutional behavior and stories are told to explain why certain people are disenfranchised and marginalized and that the "reality" makes sense. What Clarence Jordan's Cotton Patch writings do is capture the insight of culturally relevant narratives. By capturing the same power of parable that Jesus used and doing so in contemporary language, Jordan demonstrated a methodology for resisting dominant, hegemonic structures: a) telling a story; b) deconstructing a conflict saturated story (not recreating history, but deconstructing the story); and then c) creating alternative narratives that support the values that people want to live into.

I am more of a Foucault scholar than a Clarence Jordan scholar (although "scholar" would certainly be a generous description in either instance). Foucault says, "Language is an instrument of power, and people have power in society in direct proportion to their ability to participate in various discourses that shape society." Foucault's most recognized formula is "Knowledge is power and power is knowledge." But this concept is often misunderstood. What Foucault actually hopes to convey is that in any given circumstance there are multiple interpretations. The discourses of a society determine what knowledge is held to be true, right, and proper. The discourses of power become the historical, cultural metanarratives (i.e., legacy)—stories that shape (and have been shaped by) the distribution of power in society.[4] So as opposed to saying knowledge is power, it would be more accurate to say that the interpretation that gets transmitted as true is a manifestation of power.

In the case of historical harms, it is most often the case that the perpetrators of harms shape the narrative and build socializing structures (educational, social, religious, etc.) and supportive systems (political economic, legal, etc.) that conform to the narrative of justification and marginalization. In historical instances when a historically marginalized people come to power, that newly powerful group of people usually establishes a set of socializing and supporting systems that react to its previous marginalization, demonstrating cycles of victimhood and violence. Layering one set of marginalizing, isolating, and dehumanizing systems, practices and mythologies on top of a previous set adds complexity to a historical trauma because it does not undo the previously harmful legacy and its aftermath.

The narratives developed in traumagenic circumstances get incorporated into the operations of every system, patterns of relationship, and the language of a society in ways that they—over time—become the taken for granted "reality" of a society. They become the narratives that animate and constrain relationships in a culture—cultural narratives.

Cultural Narratives

A cultural narrative is a story that includes facts and beliefs, and is told from the perspective of one group to explain current disparities between groups. What are the cultural narratives in your community?

Indicator: African Americans are over-represented in the prison system

Cultural Narrative I: Many people who are African American are inherently lawless and prone to aggression. They need to be controlled by an external force or will present a danger to society. (This isn't presented here as "the truth" but rather as an example of a prevailing cultural narrative.)

Cultural Narrative II: The criminal justice system is structured to target African Americans. Prison sentences are longer for possession of drugs more common among African Americans, who are profiled, stopped more often and are more likely than people of other ethnicities to be arrested. It

---

4. Jill Freedman and Gene Combs, *Narrative Therapy: The Social Construction of Preferred Realities* (New York: W. W. Norton, 1996).

is common for African Americans to be convicted of crimes when there is little evidence of their guilt.

Clarence Jordan recognized implicitly the need to investigate and even deconstruct some of the dominant narratives and taken for granted ways of seeing the world when he said: "Even though people about us choose the path of hate and violence and warfare and greed and prejudice, we who are Christ's body must throw off these poisons and let love permeate and cleanse every tissue and cell. Nor are we to allow ourselves to become easily discouraged when love is not always obviously successful or pleasant. Love never quits, even when an enemy has hit you on the right cheek and you have turned the other, and he's also hit that."[5]

While the ideas expressed in the quote above walks the Koinonia community through truth and mercy, it leaves justice, peace and reconciliation as an unfinished work. So we ask: *What are examples of strategies or paths for harmed community members to developing safe space with their perceived or experienced oppressors to share cultural narratives that can lead to justice, peace, and reconciliation?*

Transforming historical harms at the community and cultural level requires, among other things, justice. The justice that I speak of here is not the (in)justice so often perpetrated in the legal systems. I define justice as *the establishment, restoration, and/or maintenance of a system of relationships in which everybody and everything has fundamentally equal access to the resources, systems, and relationships required for full ecosystem flourishing, group expression, and individual actualization.*

We should never forget that justice is not the same as "law and order"; in fact, I would say that often, if not always, it is the case that the demands of justice are divergent if not diametrically opposed to the workings of law and order. Many societies, particularly those organized in response to circumstances of historical harms, overwhelm a culture's ability to heal. Or those that have become traumagenic have policies, systems, rituals, practices, and relationship patterns that produce, reproduce, or reinforce marginalization and the denial of access for some groups. The discourse in these societies also reinforces the notions on inequality as appropriate or just a natural reality. What this discourse does is to lull good people into cooperating with the belief systems (ideology and hegemony) even in the ways that they seek to help. The Jordan/Koinonia approach to being in relationship sought

---

5. Clarence Jordan, *The Substance of Faith and Other Cotton Patch Sermons by Clarence Jordan,* ed. Dallas Lee (New York Association Press, 1972), 157–58.

to undermine if not undo this mindset. Jordan says: "What the poor need is not charity, but capital, not caseworkers but coworkers. And what the rich need is a wise, honorable, and just way of divesting themselves of their overabundance."[6]

In commenting on the approach that the various Koinonia communities took to dismantling the mindset of superiority even among the well-intended, Charles Marsh offered this description of the theological work of Jordan and the Kononia communities:

> The Koinonia Farm experiment, like its precursor in the Louisville Koinonia group, emerged as a result of certain exegetical decisions regarding the interpretation of the fourth chapter of *Acts*, the book in the New Testament describing the birth of the earliest Christian communities. The question Jordan had pondered as a graduate student was whether the verb tenses of verses 32–37 indicated the holding of all things in common by the disciples was a "once-and-for-all" action, or an occasional action recommended as the need arose. His seminary professor, W. O. Carver, argued that the sense of the passage favored an occasional action. "To surrender all of their goods once and for all would be to neglect the duty of responsible stewardship and to lose the discipline of administration," Carver said. Jordan heartily disagreed: the sense favors complete dispossession, not the continuing right to determine one's own actions and loyalties. Only complete dispossession is consistent with other similar purposes in the New Testament, as when Jesus instructs the rich young ruler, "If thou will be perfect, go and sell that thou hast, and give to the poor, and thou shalt have treasure in heaven." Koinonia Farm was thus built on a hermeneutical decision.[7]

This hermeneutical decision could also be understood as a counter narrative or resistance narrative against the dominant societal discourse that creates and supports the systems of separation, superiority, and scarcity. And the presence of the actual Koinonia farm and farming community stands as a physical presence and unique example to point to as an alternative to the taken for granted ways of organizing society.

Considering this hermeneutic of total surrender and shared wealth and responsibility, what is the role of economics in transforming historical harms?

6. "Letter to Friends of Koinonia, October 1968" in Millard Fuller, *Bokotola* (Piscataway, NJ: Association Press, 1977), 18.

7. Charles Marsh, *The Beloved Community: How Faith Shapes Social Justice from the Civil Rights Movement to Today* (New York: Basic Books, 2005), 67.

It is clear that one aspect of establishing right relationships that support justice is the reform of economic systems. However, economic changes without discursive changes and deconstruction or reform of other systems, rituals, patterns, and practices of relationship are either based on or supportive of the belief systems and values that ultimately result in separation and inequity. That mindset is present in all of our socializing institutions, including education systems, legal and justice systems, health care, family and even our faith systems. In 1963, Martin Luther King, Jr. famously declared that "11 o'clock Sunday morning is the most segregated hour of the week . . . And the Sunday school is still the most segregated school."

Given the probability that the organization and operation of faith communities is likely to contribute to the continuing inequity and separation, what steps can churches take toward transforming historical harms?

Churches have the opportunity to investigate the assumptions that are built into their theology that distinguishes people by race, class, ethnicity, or other variables. Churches are part of the complex web of socialization; if churches begin to create alternative narratives and counter examples in the same frame as Koinonia, then, not unlike the early church (or Koinonia Farm), they will probably experience scorn and (possibly violent) resistance. Gathering with other communities with whom they are normally separated and sharing narratives and assumptions will begin to expose the workings of some of the beliefs and how those beliefs and values shape the differentially lived experiences.

One of the great gifts of the Cotton Patch writings was the translation into present day language. By doing this, it was possible to allow the Gospels of Jesus to offer direct commentary on modern day cultural narratives. The intention of the parables was to offer a critique in a way that also provided resistance narratives for people to live into. The church has to develop a facility for developing and delivering and then living into narratives that present relationships of justice and peace.

Traumagenic circumstances have been facts of life since the dawn of time. Often the collective responses to trauma are to build trauma responses into relationship patterns, institutional and personal practices, and rituals and then reinforce the trauma response throughout all of our socializing systems. The trauma responses and the resulting marginalization and inequities become part and parcel of the fabric of society. They become the taken for granted cultural narratives that are received as reality and not as social constructions. These trauma formed narratives animate our lives, explain and justify societal inequities, and reproduce themselves through law, policy, ritual, and practice.

Changing these narratives and thus reshaping societies and relationships towards justice and peace is a long term work that requires attention to relationships at every level—individual, relational, familial, organizational, community, national and even international. Offering alternative narratives will naturally invite resistance and so the one who offers the alternative narrative will need extraordinary courage, resilience, longsuffering and a deeply held commitment to values of truth, justice, mercy, and peace.

It is a good thing we have the church as an institutional partner in this work and a good thing we have had examples like Clarence Jordan, Martin Luther King, Jr., and others to offer examples of how to tell the new narrative, live the alternative story, and invite others into the new thing that God is constantly up to.

> Then I saw a new heaven and a new earth; for the first heaven and the first earth had passed away, and the sea was no more. And I saw the holy city, the new Jerusalem, coming down out of heaven from God, prepared as a bride adorned for her husband. And I heard a loud voice from the throne saying,
>
> "See, the home of God is among mortals.
> He will dwell with them;
> they will be his peoples,
> and God himself will be with them;
> he will wipe every tear from their eyes.
> Death will be no more;
> mourning and crying and pain will be no more,
> for the first things have passed away."
> And the one who was seated on the throne said, "See, I am making all things new."
> —Revelation 21:1–5a

PART THREE

Community

8

The Kingdom Is Like Kudzu

Koinonia Farm and a New Monasticism in America

Jonathan Wilson-Hartgrove

If Clarence Jordan taught us anything, he taught that our task is to translate God's news into our own time and place. We do this, like Jesus, by enfleshing the message—turning words into deeds by the work of our hands and the grace of God, one day at a time, in scorn of the consequences. The essential thing is the demonstration plot. People need to see what God's movement looks like in practice. It is, indeed, the gospel in blue jeans.

But Clarence also knew in his gut what the philosopher Ludwig Wittgenstein said so succinctly: "words make worlds." Our capacity to imagine the kingdom that's coming is conditioned by our ability to name God's alternative now—to stand, as the apostle says, and "call those things which are not as though they were." This is why, out in the midst of those pecan trees at Koinonia Farm, there is a writing shack. It's why an agricultural missionary, when he had finished his studies at the University of Georgia, decided to go up to Louisville and learn New Testament Greek. It's why the legacy of all those homes that have been built by Habitat for Humanity and the Fuller Center for Housing depends upon the Cotton Patch

Gospels—they are imaginable because Jesus got born again in Gainsville and walked among us in the context of the Jim Crow South.

Words must be translated into deeds, for sure. But the words themselves matter. The idea must be translated into our vernacular so we can see what it means for God's new creation to break into our world here and now.

So, I want to begin with a twenty-first-century Southern paraphrase of Jesus' parable of the mustard seed. We find it amidst so many lively stories in the thirteenth chapter of Matthew's gospel. Following Clarence's example, we might read it today like this:

After driving along the state highways of Georgia, Jesus turned around and said to the folks in the back seat of his minivan, "Ya'll want to know what God's movement is like? It's like kudzu. That's some powerful stuff. Might not look like much at first—just a little Japanese weed. But it knows how to put out shoots underground, how to spread beneath the surface and weave itself into a place. Let a little bit of kudzu take root, and watch out! It'll eventually take over.

Now, where I come from, that's a parable that will preach. So you'll forgive me, I hope, if I get a little fired up here . . . I know no better way to proclaim to you what this parable of the kudzu means than to tell the story of Clarence Jordan and the Koinonia Farm. This is, of course, why we are gathered, and I cannot at this point attempt to tell you something about Clarence that you do not already know. But I do hope to reread the story we all know in a new light. I want to say that Koinonia is a rhizome shoot of God's movement in the dirt of South Georgia that makes it possible to imagine a future for Christianity in America today.

When I did my time in the seminary, I learned that a good exegete does her homework by attending to context. She puts her ear to the ground to hear what's going on before she endeavors to say what God's word means at this particular moment. Before we ask, "What shall we do?" we must ask, "What's going on?" I've stopped by today to proclaim that the kingdom is like kudzu, and I know no better way to say it than to tell you once again the story of Koinonia Farm. But if I am to tell you how Clarence shows us that the kingdom is like kudzu, I must begin by saying something about our current context. We need to spend a little time listening to what's going in American Christianity today.

The End of Christendom

Not long ago Ross Douthat, the conservative commentator who is the youngest person ever invited to be an op-ed columnist for *The New York Times*, stirred up a controversy amongst religionists in America. I'm not under any illusion that such news is at the forefront of most people's Twitter feed, so let me summarize the necessary details of this controversy.

First off, you should know this: Mr. Douthat didn't rise to his current post at *The New York Times* by writing careful and nuanced pieces of scholarship. If nothing else, he has this in common with Clarence Jordan: he is a provocateur. Which is to say, he knew he was picking a fight when he wrote a piece titled, "Can Liberal Christianity Be Saved?" the week after the Episcopal Church USA's House of Bishops met to approve a rite for the blessing of same-sex unions. Douthat noted that the broad-minded liberalism of the ECUSA has not attracted a new generation of the progressive faithful, but has coincided with a steady decline in church attendance. In short, liberal Christianity is doomed, Douthat declared, because it has cut itself off from its source by its rejection of orthodox faith and practice.

While Douthat doesn't share many sympathies with those who consider themselves liberals, he did honestly acknowledge in this piece that "the defining idea of liberal Christianity—that faith should spur social reform as well as personal conversion—has been an immensely positive force in our national life." Though he seems to think the ECUSA, along with most of mainline Christianity, is beyond redemption, Douthat holds out a prayer that liberals might find a "religious reason for their own existence."

Of course, there is another side to the story of Christendom's decline in America. If Douthat meant to pick a fight about faith, he must have expected to hear from Diana Butler Bass. For the past decade, Bass has studied and written about thriving mainline congregations for the Lilly Endowment, observing the ways that renewal is in fact happening in many corners where the light of the old Social Gospel never quite died out. More recently, in her book *Christianity After Religion*, Bass has argued that the renewal she's witnessed is part of a larger trend in American Christianity. If you pay attention to the numbers, Bass notes, it's not just liberal Christianity that's in decline. Save the influx of Latino and Asian immigrants over the past decade, conservative Christian churches would be posting greater losses than some of their mainline neighbors. Even with this influx from elsewhere, many conservative Christian organizations are cutting staff and trimming budgets. Despite the old dividing lines of the culture wars, we have more in common than we think, Bass insists. "Decline is not exclusive to the Episcopal Church, nor to liberal denominations—it is a reality facing the whole of American Christianity," she wrote in her response to Douthat.

The question, Bass says, is not simply whether liberal Christianity has a future. The question that the numbers force us to ask is whether Christianity has a future in America. For most of the past decade, national surveys about religious affiliation have consistently found the fastest growing group in the country to be the "nones"—that is, those who, when asked what religious group they identify with, answer "none." But it's not only scholars like Bass, an Episcopalian herself, who point to the decline of the attractional megachurches that have been the envy of many a mainline pastor for the past generation. In his book *The Next Evangelicalism*, the evangelical scholar Soong Chan Rah makes essentially the same point: without the addition of immigrant Christians from the global South, conservative Christianity has also been in decline for over a decade. Anyone who's honest about the numbers has to admit that things are changing.

I do not think we can understand the great transition that faith is experiencing in America apart from understanding how Constantine changed the Christian movement 1,700 years ago. The year 2012 is an important year, for it was this October, in the year 312, when the Roman Emperor understood his victory at the Milvian Bridge as the blessing of Christ. In short order, Christianity moved from being a persecuted minority movement to becoming the official religion of the Empire. Though we've been through significant political changes in the West since then, Christianity has maintained this place of privilege. Until recently, that is.

Of course, some people note that Christianity began to crumble when it turned out that Galileo was right and the earth was not, in fact, the center of the universe. Others point to Darwin or to the alliance of Germany's Reichkirche with Hitler's evil regime or to a dozen other turning points. They are all right. Christian dominance has, no doubt, suffered many blows for several hundred years. But the big change that Douthat and Bass are arguing about—the transition we are all caught up in—is the empirical evidence that says Christianity as we've known it is done.

For nearly 1,700 years in the West, you needed to be Christian to get a job downtown. This simply isn't the case anymore. After centuries of decline, we are witnessing the end of Christendom. The Christian movement has not petered out, and no one in this debate is arguing that it will any time soon. But Christianity has lost its place of privilege in the West. With it, we have lost the social power that the church in the West has so long assumed.

Seeds of Our Future in a Radical Past

The issues that are being debated in this contemporary fight about the future of Christianity—homosexuality chief among them—are important. But no single one of the issues—indeed, not every one of them put together—is as important as the question of what the Christian movement will look like after Christendom. This is the challenge facing Christianity in our time.

But we are not the first to ask this question. And this is precisely why the story of Clarence Jordan and the Koinonia Farm is so important to us now. For quite some time, Christendom has had its critics. But the most radical—and, I think, the most promising—critique of Christendom is that tradition that has resisted it from its beginnings. It is no accident that the monastic movement began in the deserts of Egypt 1,700 years ago, at precisely the same moment when Constantine was laying the foundations of Christendom. Those desert ammas and abbas who fled the city to discover a new way of life with Jesus in the wilderness were the founders of a radical resistance tradition that has run parallel to the institutional church's alliance with political power in the West.

The seeds of our future, I want to say, were sown in this radical past. In the fourth century, the monastic rejection of mainstream life in the cities was not a rejection of the world per se. Asceticism was not, as it has sometimes been misunderstood, a hatred of embodied life in God's creation. It was, instead, a radical affirmation of the good life we're called to in Christ and community. Likewise, the monastic vow of poverty was not a denial of our material need as creatures. It was a prophetic witness to a church that was tempted to worship Mammon. Poverty was a way of remembering that Jesus taught us we cannot serve both God and Money.

Clarence Jordan and the Koinonia Farm experiment are, to my mind, an embodiment of this radical tradition. Their commitments to interracialism, pacifism, a common purse, and shared life in community cannot be understood simply as principled convictions. They are, rather, prophetic commitments meant to contradict the American church's idolatry of racism, militarism, avarice, and individualism.

One of my favorite of Clarence's prophetic quips is his response to the pastor who showed him around his million dollar church, pointing out that the cross alone cost them $10,000. "Brother, you got gypped," Clarence said. "Time was when Christians could get one of them for free." Like the prophet Amos, Clarence Jordan cried out against the injustice of ostentatious wealth as an offense not only to the poor, but also to the God who became poor in Jesus. But Clarence instinctively knew that it wasn't enough to just say that the church was getting gypped in its worship of Mammon. Like the monastic tradition before him, Clarence knew that some of Jesus' followers—especially those who were tempted by Mammon—would have to renounce personal property as a living witness to the power of the cross.

And so it was that some Christian radicals planted a shoot of kingdom kudzu in south Georgia soil. They did not have the power to overthrow Jim Crow. But they could live, in one place, as if Jim Crow had already died. In their bones they knew that Jim Crow could not last any more than our addiction to Mammon can. They cannot last because they are not true to the way God made the universe. Clarence knew, as the Mennonite historian John Howard Yoder later put it, that "those who carry crosses work with the grain of the universe." Our hope is nothing short of resurrection.

Which brings me back to kudzu. I don't have the credentials Clarence had when it comes to agriculture, but my brother and I did start a landscaping business back in our hometown when we were young. I maintain my certification in weed, grass, and pest control in the state of North Carolina. I might not have a green thumb, but I know weeds. And weeds point us toward the future of Christianity, I think. Because if you've ever tried to tend a garden or keep a lawn, you know there are some weeds—those big suckers with a thick stem—that grow up almost overnight. They can easily grow taller than me, mocking every efforts to keep a yard looking nice. But those big, fast growing weeds aren't very smart. They're like a high steepled church with a $10,000 cross. They look big and strong, but their roots are so short and shallow that you can pluck them out of the flower bed with a single pull.

The weeds that have staying power—the ones that will take over a garden—are the rhizomes. Usually their stems are small, if they have any stems at all, and it's easy to knock them down with a weed-eater. But rhizomes spread through an underground root structure, thriving beneath the surface and growing stronger all the time. There's really no way to get rid of them unless you tear up a whole yard. Fact of the matter is, they always win in the end.

Kudzu is a rhizome. An "invasive species," they call it. If it gets its root system in the soil, it will take over a whole forest. It will, in the words of the prophet Daniel, grow into a "mountain that covers the whole earth." To say that the kingdom is like kudzu is to say that the end of Christendom, however troubling it might be to some, is good news for all of us. Because now the kudzu has room to thrive.

Thanks be to God, little groups like Koinonia got the roots of God's movement into this soil long ago. If we pay attention, we can trace the web of shoots beneath the surface to Habitat and the Fuller Center, to Jubilee Partners and to the Open Door Community, to the Prison and Jail Project—and all of this in Georgia. We can trace it on up to North Carolina, to the Rutba House community where I live. Just recently, we learned that a group of folks lived in Christian community in our neighborhood back in the 1970s—just two streets over from where we started in 2003. Where did they get the idea? Koinonia Farm.

A new monasticism is stirring across the land as people who are disappointed with the forms of church that they've known opt out of old structures to follow hard after Jesus with their whole lives in small discipleship communities. The religionists are right: Christendom is dying and its institutions are in decline. But God's movement is getting born again in America, and it's spreading like kudzu. The seeds of our future are in our radical past. Which is to say, Koinonia matters. What we're here to talk about isn't just fascinating history. It's the future of Christianity in America.

9

Tearing Down Walls

Shane Claiborne

I am thrilled and honored to be a part of this whole weekend celebration. We've got so much wisdom in this room! It's a gift to be with friends and hear their stories.

When I started thinking about what Clarence Jordan and Koinonia have meant to me, I was struck by how it's one of those communities that has been tearing down walls and sort of doing some holy trespassing over the layers of walls that we build with each other. So I wanted to start with a Scripture that meant a lot to me and is really appropriate given the life of Clarence and Koinonia. It's the story that is familiar to many of us—it's the rich man and Lazarus from Luke 16. I'm going to read this old story.

> There was a rich man who was dressed in purple and fine linen and he lived in luxury every day. At his gate was laid a beggar named Lazarus, covered in sores, and longing to eat what fell from the rich man's table. Even the dogs came and licked the man's sores. Well the time came and the beggar died. The angels carried him to Abraham's side. The rich man also died and was buried. In Hell, where he was in torment, the rich man looked up and saw Abraham far away with Lazarus by his side. So he called to him, "Father Abraham! Have pity on me and send Lazarus to dip the tip of his finger in water and cool my tongue because I am in agony in this

fire." But Abraham replied, "Son, remember that in your lifetime, you received your good things while Lazarus received bad things. But now he is comforted here and you are in agony. And besides all of this, there is a great chasm that has been fixed so that those who want to go from here to you cannot, nor can anyone cross over from you to us."

I know that's one of those stories that kind of ruins the chi in the room; it's a heavy story. But I think what the parables do is they invite us to write a different ending to the story with our lives, kind of like those movies where you get the alternate ending if you want it. This story kind of provokes that in us in saying that it doesn't have to end that way. I think of Koinonia and Clarence and I think they are people who have been writing a gospel ending to the story saying, "It doesn't have to end that way." I once heard it said that the true gospel, when we hear it, should comfort the disturbed and disturb the comfortable. That's what this story does to us.

I think the early Christians, like Saint John Chrysostom, the golden-mouthed preacher, loved this story. And one of the things they point out is that there's this peculiar thing happening with the names. The rich man doesn't have a name—he's just the rich man. But the poor man, Lazarus, he has a name. And incidentally, Lazarus is the only person who's given a name in any of the parables of Jesus. And they said there's something to that. What they go on to point out is that the rich man on earth, he probably had a name and I'll bet people knew that name. He was on boards and plaques, and probably had a corporation named after him. People knew his name. But the poor man, like so many of our brothers and sisters in the world, is living and dying with nobody knowing his name or her name and yet in the story "Lazarus" means *the one God rescued*.

That poor man now is next to Abraham, sitting next to God. You also get the sense in the story that, and St. John says, that the rich guy was a religious guy. He knows the story. He says, "Father Abraham!" He identifies with the story, yet his religion did nothing to tear down the wall, to get to know the pain and the suffering just on the other side. He comes to find out that the chasm that he has between the gated neighborhood he found himself in, not only did it separate himself from the poor and the suffering but it separated him from God.

Isn't that true, that in all our picket fences and our cubicles and all the ways that we insulate ourselves, we think that we're locking people out, but we're actually locking ourselves in? And we find that we're lonely people because we're robbed of compassion and that's what we're made for. So we end up very rich and lonely people.

And then there are folks like Clarence and Koinonia and all these folks that teach us the possibility of seeing what's on the other side of the wall. It strikes me how good in the church we all are at building walls and excluding people; Doctor King saying that the most segregated hour is 11:00 on Sunday morning. I grew up in east Tennessee in the Bible Belt, where I saw some beautiful things, but I also saw some of the ways we can exclude. I remember hearing a story growing up about a homeless guy that came to worship on Sunday morning. He came to the real wealthy congregation wearing all of his street clothes and carrying his bags with him. He plopped down up front and everybody sort of looked at him like he didn't belong. Then the pastor came up and said, "Sir, I don't know if you've been here before, but this is the house of God. So I want you to do something. I want you to go out and ask God this week what you should wear when you come to church." The homeless guy left before the service even started, really awkwardly, feeling like he didn't belong. A week passed and the next Sunday the guy came back same as he had before, wearing all his street clothes, carrying his bags with him—it's the only way he rolled, you know? He came in again, sat down up front and the pastor said, "Sir, I recognize you. And I asked you to do something. Did you ask God what you should wear?" And the guy said, "Yeah! I did, Pastor, and he said he didn't know 'cause he's never been to your church."

I think of how, so often, we've become known for who we've excluded than who we've embraced; more for what we're against than what we're for. A study a few years ago by the Barna Research Group, kind of the Gallup of Christianity, they went to every state in the U.S. and they asked young non-Christians, "What are your perceptions of Christians?" The number one answer was that Christians are anti-gay. That was the number-one answer: anti-homosexual. Number two was that Christians are judgmental; number three was that Christians are hypocrites. I'll stop there, because the list doesn't get much better. And yet, I'm so encouraged because I think that there is a movement happening in the church that's drawing wisdom from communities like Koinonia and folks like Clarence and Florence and Dorothy Day, all those folks who have mirrored this idea that indeed, we are to become these places that mirror, that demonstrate, the kingdom of God on Earth.

I thought I might share a couple of stories that are not from Georgia, where I've been able to see that. When I moved up to Philly, we began to see a lot of ugly laws that our city was passing that did exactly what this story does, that excluded and ostracized especially the homeless folks in Philadelphia. In fact more than fifty cities in the United States have passed anti-homeless legislation, terrible laws that specifically and selectively target homeless folks. For instance, some of the laws make trash city property, so if a homeless person is found trying to find some clothes or food or cardboard, they can be arrested or cited for stealing from city property. They're just terrible laws.

But one of the laws in Philadelphia made it illegal to distribute food. So ten years ago, we began to protest those laws. We had worship services in the parks where we would give out communion, which was very controversial, since you weren't allowed to distribute food. Then after communion, we would bring in pizzas, which was even a little bit more controversial. We ended up going to jail and winning in court over that. But this last year, that same law reared its ugly face again and the mayor of Philadelphia passed an executive order in the city of Philadelphia that it's illegal to share food with more than three people in public. So we began these public hearings where what was so beautiful was that the people that came out of the woodwork was the church! We had Pentecostals, Catholics, Mennonites, Quakers, and the Occupy movement and all kinds of different folks working together, but especially the church and people of faith were coming out. Hundreds of us voiced opposition to this executive order that made it illegal to share food. What was amazing was that you had this old, Pentecostal church-lady who got up and she said, "Eleven years ago, God told me to start making casseroles and taking them out to the homeless. So I did. Every Thursday night I'd make casseroles and take them down to the Parkway and give them out to folks on the street. I haven't missed a Thursday in eleven years. If the mayor wants to stop that, then the mayor better talk to God, 'cause God started it all."

Then a Catholic theologian stood up and said, "We have a fundamental problem with this executive order because for us, to feed the homeless is to feed Christ. It's a sacrament. When Jesus said that when you do it unto the least of these, you do it unto me, we are feeding Christ. So if you say we can't feed the homeless, you're saying we cannot feed Christ. And it's also a violation of religious freedom."

A federal court upheld that decision and blocked that executive order, so now we're allowed to feed people in Philadelphia. What was beautiful was seeing the church *be* the church and demonstrate the justice and love and compassion of God in a city that was continuing to segregate and lock out those who were most vulnerable.

One of my friends in Philly was telling me that his congregation during this same period began to welcome homeless folks. The City came in, and since there were folks that were sleeping in the building, they said, "You're not set up to run a shelter, so we want you to know that we're going to shut this down. You don't have proper licensing and permits." And the church folks, these guys were Pentecostals, and you don't mess with the Pentecostals, they said, "Well, we're going to pray about it so let's meet back in a week." So they met back with the City a week later and they said, "We've prayed about what you said, that we can't run a shelter, so we won't call it a shelter, we'll call it a church, and what the church does is welcome people, anybody. And if you want to try to shut it down, then we dare you." The news came out and what they said publicly in a press conference was, "We're not running a shelter, we're having a revival. And every night, the revival starts at about 8:00 and goes till the next morning. Anybody is welcome!" I went one night. It was beautiful. For two hours, we sang songs, people shared their stories, and we had communion together. After about two hours, one of the pastors said, "All right, that concludes the formal service of the revival. The next eight hours will be silent meditation. Everybody have a good night!"

I praise God for that holy and humble defiance that I see in Philadelphia and that I see in the history of Koinonia. I see that holy defiance on the border of the U.S. and Mexico where we visited a community that began a new sanctuary movement of welcoming immigrants. They were deeply concerned about the immigration crisis, as many of us are. They said, "We refuse to let politicians in D.C. legislate how we should treat the alien and the stranger in the land." They said, "We'll read Leviticus, we'll read the Bible and see that we have a God that is constantly making outsiders insiders and teaching us to love the strangers as if they were our own flesh and blood." So they started doing that. They had Sanctuary Houses and told us about worship services they would organize on the border. They would walk to the wall; they would have Christians living in Mexico that would walk to the wall and Christians living on the U.S. side who would walk to the wall. They would gather on both sides of the wall and they would sing songs to each other and worship God together and then to close the service off, they would serve each other communion by throwing bread over the wall. It's not very Catholic, but I love it! There's something beautiful about it that points toward the image that we see that the walls will not prevail; the gates will not prevail. We have a God that is tearing down the walls that we've built and the more walls we have the more lonely we become and the further from God we become.

Probably one of the most walled areas of the world is in the Holy Land, right where so many unholy things happen, so many heartbreaking things. My mom and I got to go to the West Bank and through Israel and Palestine. As we were there, you'd see these images along the wall. Some of the images that are painted along the wall, they show the possibility of seeing who's on the other side. We heard these incredible stories.

On one of those trips, we got to visit families that are doing reconciliation. One of the Palestinian Christians, Sami Awad, said, "Something strange happened. I felt the Spirit moving me to understand the Jewish pain. That was a hard call for me, but I went to Germany and I went to Auschwitz and I went to the Holocaust museums and I began to study the history of the Jewish people. I began to have new eyes as I looked at the wall. Now I look at the wall as a Palestinian Christian, and I don't just see hatred. That's what I used to see. Now I see fear. It's a fear that I can understand, but it's not a fear that justifies the wall, don't get me wrong. But now I see the possibility of breaking through that wall and seeing these people on the other side."

I'm reminded of another community that we visited in that same land, the Tent of Nations, the Nassar Family Farm. It's one of those beautiful stories of reconciliation: a farm that looks a lot like Koinonia. They lived on this land that for them has been passed on from generation to generation, but the Israeli settlers began to move around the land and began to try to take their land from them. And unlike many Palestinian families, the Nassar family actually had the deeds from their land that showed that they owned it. So they went to court, and as they fought it through court, after ten years it became pretty clear that their land couldn't be taken legally. So the settlers began to still move in around it and began to harass the Nassar Family. They dumped a bunch of boulders in their driveway, the only way that you could get into their farm. They began to uproot the olive trees. But the Nassars said, "We continue to pray and work for the walls to come down." They painted this beautiful mural on the side of their farm that says, "*We refuse to be your enemies.*" It's that defiance that's led them to bring in Jewish folks who replanted the olive trees and who have helped them to build that little farm.

Then the Israeli government said, "OK, you may own the land, but you don't have a right to build any buildings or have any utilities," so they totally went all permaculture, like the Koinonia folks! They went off the grid, they built their buildings underground, they used solar energy, they recycled rainwater. One of my friends asked them how they found the courage to do this. And with the biggest smile in the world, Daoud Nassar said, "Jesus."

One of the women in the Nassar family told us the story of one of the settler women that she's gotten to know. She invited this Israeli settler to her home for dinner on the family farm. As soon as she came in and walked into the little underground hut with no running water, this Israeli settler, this woman, she just began to weep. She cried, "This is so unfair. On the other side of the wall, we've got swimming pools and heated water and you don't even have running water." There was a moment where a little crack in the wall appeared. You could see the possibility of humanizing that person whose name we haven't known. It's the invitation of stories like these, the story of Koinonia, that promise us that the walls will not prevail; that we have a God that has a history of tearing down walls and reconciling the most unlikely people.

That's one of the things I love about the dinner table of Jesus: you've got a Roman tax collector and a Zealot revolutionary—unlikely friends! Zealots kill tax collectors for fun on weekends! But they're together and everybody is invited to be a new creation! Jesus is challenging the sword of the Zealots and he's challenging the tax-collecting system of the Romans and inviting everybody to have new eyes and become a new creation, to reorient our lives around Christ. And that should give all of us hope.

I was in Texas, and this guy came up to me and said, "I'm a redneck. I'm a textbook redneck. You know, gun-totin', pick-up truck-driving redneck. But I've been reading your books and that got me reading the Bible again. I was reading the gospel again. And it has all messed me up. So you pray for me, 'cause I'm a recovering redneck." How beautiful that we're all recovering from something. That's the grace Koinonia has demonstrated to me and to us: no one is beyond redemption. The love and grace of God tears down walls so much so that both the persecuted and the persecutors are set free. The gate and the wall were neither good for Lazarus nor the rich man, so let 'em fall.

Nora Tisdale—The Local Theology and Folk Art
of Clarence Jordan's Preaching (Volume I)

Vincent Harding—Loving Respect, Clear Disagreement (Volume I)

Charles Marsh—At Work in the Fields of the Lord:
Clarence Jordan as Prophet of Radical Ordinariness (Volume I)

Ted Swartz – Rooted in the Cotton Patch Interview (Volume II)

President Jimmy Carter—Opening Remarks (Volumes I and II)

Sam Mahone—Reflections on the Americus Movement (Volume I)

Shane Claiborne—Tearing Down Walls (Volume II)

PART FOUR

Agriculture, Housing, and Stewardship

10

Koinonia Farm and the Permaculture Movement

Wayne Weiseman

Good afternoon, everyone. I want to give you some background to show you what is happening at Clarence's place, what's the theory behind it, what's the essence behind the system that Koinonia Farm is putting together.

Clarence and Florence Jordan and Martin and Mabel England began their experiment in Christian living on a farm—growing food. That experiment continues today and the farming practice the community has chosen to follow is called permaculture. The word *permaculture* was coined in 1978 by Bill Mollison, an Australian ecologist, and one of his students, David Holmgren. It is a contraction of "permanent agriculture" or "permanent culture."

On my way down here I was thinking a lot about the word *agriculture* and the word *permaculture*, some of the terminology that we use as a culture, that we've grown up with, and how some of it is just false. I'm from Illinois, and it's considered the breadbasket of the country. But they're not really producing enough wheat for it to be the breadbasket of the country. It's mostly soy and corn that gets shipped to hogs in North Carolina, and then the pork gets shipped back to Illinois to be sold in supermarkets. So breadbasket? I don't think so anymore. Maybe at one time in the history of agriculture in the Midwest this was true, but I don't think it holds true anymore.

The word *agriculture* has its roots in the word *culture*, which either meant to till the land or to care for the land. And then *agri* comes from a Latin root that means "field." So *agriculture* either means to till the fields or to care for the fields. Bill Mollison, the creator of permaculture, coined the word in the 1970s to mean "permanent agriculture," meaning that he wanted us to develop perennial systems rather than strictly annual systems, although under such a comprehensive system as permaculture, annual crops are just fine. But one of the goals is to shoot for perennial systems. Here's an example: if you plant an acre of chestnuts, as opposed to an acre of corn, you'll get ten times the biomass from an acre of chestnuts and just as many functions from chestnuts as you will from corn. Additionally, chestnuts contain similar nutrients and starches that you find in rice. But because of the fact that we've grown up a certain way and we have very specific tastes, and that the powers that be have placed them in the marketplace for us, we wouldn't even consider the chestnut as an excellent protein- and mineral-rich flour that we could use in place of standard flour. That's just one small example.

According to Bill Mollison, the originator of the permaculture design system,

> Permaculture principles focus on thoughtful designs for small-scale intensive systems, which are labor efficient and which use biological resources instead of fossil fuels. Designs stress ecological connections and closed energy and material loops. The core of Permaculture is design and the working relationships and connections between all things. Each component in a system performs multiple functions, and each function is supported by many elements. Key to efficient design is observation and replication of natural ecosystems, where designers maximize diversity with polycultures, stress efficient energy planning for houses and settlement, using and accelerating natural plant succession, and increasing the highly productive edge-zones within the system.

Permaculture is about designing ecological human habitats and food production systems. It is a land use and community building movement that strives for the harmonious integration of human dwellings, microclimate, annual and perennial plants, animals, soils, and water into stable, productive communities. The focus is not on these elements themselves, but rather on the relationships created among them by the way we place them in the landscape. This synergy is further enhanced by mimicking patterns found in nature.

A central theme in permaculture is the design of ecological landscapes that produce food. Emphasis is placed on multi-use plants, cultural practices such as sheet mulching and trellising, and the integration of animals to recycle nutrients and graze weeds. However, permaculture entails much more than just food production. Energy-efficient buildings, wastewater treatment, recycling, and land stewardship in general are other important components of permaculture. More recently, permaculture has expanded its purview to include economic and social structures that support the evolution and development of more permanent communities. As such, permaculture design concepts are applicable to urban as well as rural settings, and are appropriate for single households as well as whole farms, villages, towns, and cities.

Since our emergence as a species, humankind has gone through three great cultural epochs, each with its prototypical lifestyle forms and folkways. The first epoch was that of the pre-agricultural tribe of hunter-gatherers and primitive cultivators. Hunter-gatherer societies sustained themselves by having an intimate and intuitive knowledge of their surroundings. They acted as "gardeners" in the natural world and walked the earth quietly, leaving as little trace of their presence as possible.

The simultaneous development of agriculture ten thousand years ago in various regions of the world gave birth to the second cultural epoch. The ability to grow food year after year from seeds and cultivated plants selected for vigor and reliability gave the former hunter-gatherer the opportunity to remain in one place and cultivate extensive food crops for sustenance for family, relatives, and friends.

The third cultural epoch gave rise to an explosion of intellectual, artistic, and scientific learning. The technological discoveries and inventions of this era (which is still with us) helped to disassemble nature into pieces and then reassemble them into mechanical entities.

We now stand at a time when the best of these three great epochs must come together to help create an ecologically sound environment for all. The ecological epoch will see a re-sacralization of the living world in which life forms are more than resources—they are also our relatives. The new epoch will not reject science or technology but bring them into a context where phenomena are understood as parts of a systemic whole that includes the spirit of the whole.

What Bill Mollison did was, rather than thinking of permanent agriculture, he now took the *agri* out and called it "permanent culture," because we're not strictly dealing with agriculture per se, but the built environment, the waste stream, the biological systems, energy systems, and animals. So it became more of an all-encompassing lifestyle. It's not what I hear from a lot of people now: "we're going to permaculture our backyard." It's much larger than that. We're not interested in putting a photovoltaic system on a house and saying that we're "doing permaculture." What we do is look at the entire property and think about first of all, what's there—what are the natural forces that are circulating through the property and what is leaving the property? What we try to do is make use of these forces plus what we call "the biological intelligence" of the region.

In biological systems there is no waste. Everything is recycled and reused for the continuance of life that is happening cyclically over and over and over again.

In the culture that we've developed we have created all kinds of gadgets and toys for ourselves—and I'm part of it; I'm not putting it down because the technology we've developed is absolutely brilliant and we couldn't just throw it all out the door. We try, in permaculture, to open all that up. We say that the problem is the solution. So in the issues and constraints that we've created for ourselves, we're trying to look at it for what it is and either transform it into something that brings health to a landscape or to find an alternative, to look back into other cultures and find ways to bring that into our culture and develop a balanced landscape, both for ourselves and all the other creatures that move about our landscape.

The big question for me is, how do we transition from the agriculture of central Illinois, a single crop like soybeans, to something like a farm, for example, up in Wisconsin, where they're growing hazelnuts, but in between the hazelnuts they're growing a whole variety of crops until the hazelnut trees become mature and they can take a crop off the hazelnut trees. There are about eighty different species of crops that are growing at the particular Wisconsin farm. It's one of the most beautiful farms I've ever visited. If we think out how to place these crops in the landscape based on landform and climate and rainfall averages—this all works.

In permaculture, it's a design system. There is an inverse relationship between planning and work. We say that if you take 100 hours to design, the result will be only an hour of work. I know from many years of experience that if I think through something for only an hour, it's going to take me 100 hours of work. I've been through it too many times! And when permaculture first showed up in the 1970s, and Bill Mollison's big book *Permaculture: A Designer's Manual* came out on the market, it blew my mind. I had been into all of these different things and it put it all together for me.

So it's a system, that if you want to jump in, I really recommend it. It's a very general and comprehensive way of looking at the world, how to produce high yields for ourselves, but also how to care for the earth and care for people and to redistribute the wealth of the harvest. Going through all the literature of the past thirty years, I have yet to come across something as comprehensive as this.

So how do we get away from the monocultural, one crop at a time model, with all the hedgerows ripped out and replaced with fenceline, going on for thousands of acres? I was driving down to Texas a few years ago to teach and I was going through Arkansas. I looked over and they were doing the cotton harvest. And there was nobody in the tractor! This thing was moving along on the land. It was run by a GPS. I thought to myself that this is very absurd, that we've come to the point where we don't even get in the tractor, let alone get out of it and go and feel what the soil is like. We are that far removed.

One of the other things that permaculture looks at is that we would like to get back to working with small, intensive systems. There are twenty-eight million acres of back and front yards in America. I want you to try to conceive of what that means. Just think of an acre: 53,000 and some square feet. Multiply that by twenty-eight million. I was working on a farm up until two years ago in Illinois, a farm that I had managed for fifteen years. I retired two years ago because my body was falling apart—it was too work intensive. It was strictly an organic farm, a market farm, but now I'm working on my sixth of an acre in town and in the first year, my family and I produced 50 percent of our food needs. Yes, it can be done. By stacking many functions together, utilizing horizontal and vertical space, we can insert many plant species in the thousands of niches that we find in a landscape. We are so accustomed to broad scale, monocultural "farms" across thousands of acres that we cannot break the habit: crops in neat, linear rows, behemoth tractors stirring the soil and injecting seeds, harvest with nary a human hand close to the plants being harvested.

How does all of this "permaculture" way of seeing the world merge with the profound thought and perspective of one Clarence Jordan? And how does the work that all the folks at Koinonia Farm are doing today reflect the permaculture way?

Clarence Jordan originally set up Koinonia as a farming community. The production of food for all is the essence of service. Currently, Koinonia has diversified into raising not only plant-based crops, but also animals: meat, milk, and eggs. This combination of plant and animal nutrition covers all the bases and supports the overall health of the community. It affords those that come to visit Koinonia and those that join the community the opportunity to immerse themselves in the farming operation. With the majority of people living in cities in the current culture, the need for experienced and knowledgeable farmers and growers is becoming more apparent.

Because of the fact that permaculture can be put into practice no matter the scale, no matter whether it is rural, suburban or urban, no matter if it is practiced on two thousand acres or on the thirtieth floor of an apartment building in the center of the city, it has come to represent "the" alternative to the status quo: the industrial farm, the monocultural mindset, whether it's growing food or building housing on a city block. Permaculture purports things done on a human scale, a scale that we can all participate in without reliance on the corporate powers that be.

In essence, Koinonia Farm is a harbinger looking toward the future of humanity. But it is not only the future that it looks toward, because how can the future become the future if, in the present, the work is not being done? Permaculture principles and methodologies are its bread and butter, implemented through rigorous thinking, hard work, and soul. Permaculture is a perfect marriage of community, good food, and an all-encompassing, whole systems approach. May we all take a lesson from this marriage going on at Koinonia Farm and learn to serve.

11

The History and Future of Partnership Housing

David Snell

During that last, eventful week of Jesus' ministry he visited the home of Simon the leper in Bethany. A woman came and anointed his head with costly oil, a wasteful act to the disciples who thought the more practical thing would have been to sell the oil and give the money to the poor. But Jesus said to leave her alone, that he was soon departing and, in one of those enigmatic quips that make the Bible so challenging, said, "For ye have the poor always with you."

Throughout his ministry Jesus taught that those with more should share with those with less. In the simple story that haunts good Christians he told the wealthy young man that the way to salvation was for him to sell all of his things and give the money to the poor. "If you have two coats," he'd say, "give one to the man with none." But against all that good counsel was the simple observation there will always be the poor.

And he was right. Now, 2,000 years later, we live in a world where the majority of people live in poverty. A billion people go to bed each night in hovels and shacks. Hunger, illness, and boredom are the realities of life for countless people around the world. And yet the resources exist for all of God's people to have a decent place to live, enough food to eat, and something interesting to do. Two questions, then, immediately come to mind: Why is this so and how can we fix it?

The whys of poverty are complex and include a wide range of causes, from politics to weather. In too many cases poverty is an inherited condition, a mindset. Remarkably, though, we live in an age when technology and resources could well come together to provide all people with the means to lead lives of dignity, freed of the shackles of poverty. Clarence Jordan identified the problem clearly in his October 1968 letter, where he laid out the plan for the Fund for Humanity. He wrote, "It has also become clear to us that as man has lost his identity with God he has lost it with his fellow man."

It was with a hope of restoring that identity with God and our fellow man that the Fund for Humanity was born, a new economic model in which those with resources could share with those in need in a thoughtful, efficient way. In that same October letter Clarence wrote, "What the poor need is not charity, but capital, not caseworkers but co-workers. And what the rich need is a wise, honorable and just way of divesting themselves of their overabundance." The Fund for Humanity would meet both of these needs.

The three pillars of the plan were partnership farming, partnership industries, and partnership housing. The idea for each was that the Fund would provide the basic resource—land, equipment, and capital. The partners, the Koinonia community and their poor neighbors, would provide the human resource and together they would raise food, create products, and have a decent place to rest their heads each night. With interest-free cash from the Fund for Humanity the poor would be better positioned to grow and process their own food and compete in the marketplace. At the same time they would be able to help build and own a simple, decent home. What was at work here was a new and practical sort of charity. Clarence wrote, "The Fund will give away no money. It is not a handout. It will provide capital for the partnership enterprises." An unstated purpose of the partnership model was that the dignity of all those who participated would be retained, indeed enhanced. By making capital available to the poor one of their most significant barriers to prosperity was lifted.

The importance of the partnership concept to charitable giving can't be overstated. To many, charity means that those with surplus give to those in need, but in that transaction is a serious flaw. The very act of giving creates an imbalance between the two parties—the giver, by his simple ability to give, is superior to the recipient, who, for whatever reason, cannot provide for himself. There are times when this is necessary—disasters, famine, and sickness all produce conditions where those who have are called by simple human decency to provide for those who don't.

In too many cases, though, simple giving has unintended consequences, creating dependencies, robbing the recipients of dignity and a sense of self-worth, stealing initiative and the will, and sometimes the ability, for the recipients to care for themselves. Entire nations have fallen victim to this imbalance—Haiti, for example, which has been on the receiving end of so much simple charity over the years that it no longer functions as a productive society. Government welfare programs can create this same unhealthy imbalance.

The genius of the partnership concept is that it maintains the balance. "The Fund will give away no money. It is not a handout." Recipients of the Fund's capital work for it. In the case of housing, the partner families help build their home and then they pay the cost, over time with no interest charged or profit made. The point, though, is that the recipient of the "charity" is a full partner in the transaction, and, in the case of housing, at the end they own the house that they paid for and helped build.

Further, the house payments go back into the Fund for Humanity to help build and renovate more houses, thus turning the recipient of the capital into a donor in his own right. Jesus said that it is more blessed to give than to receive, but the poor seldom have the opportunity to have the greater blessing. Partnership housing gives them that opportunity. This is an elegant and transformative type of charity.

Millard Fuller was a part of the group that developed the partnership plan, and he was drawn to the housing component. It was to this that he dedicated his life, his vast fundraising and promotional talents and, in the process, helped redefine charitable giving. Through Habitat for Humanity he made decent shelter a reality for millions, and through the Fuller Center for Housing he refocused his energy on the basic tenets of that early plan. Partnership housing has been a success, although a good deal has been learned along the way.

The first houses were built on two subdivisions laid out on Koinonia Farm. Clarence Jordan didn't live to see the first house, Bo and Emma Johnson's, built, and theirs is a great story. Bo signed the mortgage with an "X" as he never learned to read or write. The Johnsons raised five children in that house—one went on to be a New York attorney. There was a great celebration when the Johnsons burned their mortgage. Bo and Emma lived in that house the rest of their lives and became the first partnership housing success story.

Millard and Linda left the Farm after that to test the philosophy in Mbandaka, Zaire (now the Democratic Republic of Congo), where over 500 houses were built at a place called Bokotola. Mbandaka was a Belgian outpost and has fallen on hard times over the years, but Bokotola remains to this day a peaceful enclave of well-kept houses and laughing children. Another success story.

Not every partnership house has a happy ending. Often the poor are trapped because they simply don't know how to manage money—understandable if they've never had much money to manage. Many times they lack basic knowledge of how to maintain the house. A certain level of discipline attends homeownership, and one of the lessons learned is that creating successful homeownership often requires training in the basics of money management and home maintenance.

A third essential element for success is the willingness of the recipient to do what is necessary to succeed, and this is the greatest challenge. Without a change of behavior and attitude people continue the same destructive habits that keep them trapped in poverty. People who have lived their life in poverty, and who may come from generations of poverty, need to be reminded that success is something they can aspire to. It is in this that the human flaw that Clarence sought to correct finds expression.

"It has also become clear to us that as man has lost his identity with God he has lost it with his fellow man," wrote Clarence. Perhaps a step towards reestablishing that identity with God might be reestablishing an identity with his fellow man, and an opportunity for that lies in the partnership housing model. A Fuller Center build, for example, brings a wide variety of good-hearted souls together for a common purpose. Rich and poor, black and white, Catholics and Baptists put any differences they might have aside in order to get a house built with a family in need. The most visible product of partnership housing is the house, but perhaps the most significant product lies in the relationships that form as people of good will reach out to those in need and lift them up. The engagement with the partner family will begin well before the build and last well after it. The local Fuller Center covenant partner's family nurture committee will work with the family to secure appropriate financial counseling, train them in household maintenance, and be with them through the trials that will surely follow.

The volunteers and partner family will have many opportunities to reestablish that lost identity.

So what of the future of partnership housing? Throughout most of his forty year ministry Millard Fuller provided decent shelter by building new houses. This is still true in the developing world where housing is in short supply. But here in the United States, where there are millions of vacant houses, The Fuller Center is moving toward rehabilitation work. By taking existing housing stock and repairing it, upgrading as necessary, derelict properties are restored, neighborhoods enhanced, and waste reduced. In the process the local tax base is increased and, when properties are acquired from lending institutions their "toxic asset" problem is solved and Community Reinvestment Act requirements met. And a family gets a decent place where they can make a home.

Whether it's new construction or renovation work, the basic purposes of partnership housing are being met—people have an opportunity to renew their identity with God and with their fellow man; capital is made available to the poor; and the rich have a wise, honorable, and just way of divesting themselves of their overabundance. Everyone is enriched and ennobled, which is just what Jesus is looking for us to do.

12

Faster, Stronger, and More Aggressive

Is Habitat Really A Shoot from the Stump of Clarence?

―――⊳●⊲―――

Joe Gatlin

"A shoot shall come out from the stump of Jesse, and a branch shall grow out of his roots. The spirit of the Lord shall rest on him, the spirit of wisdom and understanding, the spirit of counsel and might, the spirit of knowledge and the fear of the Lord."
Isaiah 11:1–2

"Day by day, as they spent much time together in the temple, they broke bread at home and ate their food with glad and generous hearts."
Acts 2:46

A Personal Letter from Clarence Jordan to Friends of Koinonia, October 21, 1968

> For several years it has been clear that Koinonia stands at the end of an era or perhaps its existence. Its goals and methods which were logical and effective in the 1940's and 50's seem no longer relative to an age which is undergoing vast and rapid changes. An integrated, Christian community was a very practical vehicle through which to bear witness to a segregated society a decade ago, but now it is too slow, too weak, not aggressive enough. Its lack of mobility gives it the appearance of a house on the bank of a river as the rushing torrents of history swirl by.[1]

A Funeral for Intentional Christian Community?

"Too slow, too weak, not aggressive enough." "No longer relative." "At the end of an era or perhaps its existence." "No longer valid."

Ouch, Clarence! That's harsh!

To my knowledge no one ever accused Clarence of pulling his punches or being subtle. Clarence was a master at using a pithy phrase or a well-constructed paragraph to distill the truth, clarify direction, and draw a line in the sand. Why use nuance when people need to get off the fence?

As an adherent and supporter of Habitat for Humanity I love this letter. It is practically canon for Habitat; it is our genesis, essentially our charter. "Revere" is not too strong of a word to describe the relationship of especially us Habitat oldtimers with this text. Concepts and taglines familiar to all Habitat adherents, new and old, such as "not a handout but a hand-up," "no interest," and "what the poor need is not charity, but capital, not case-workers, but co-workers," are found here.

However, as someone who has lived in Christian community all of my adult life, I cringe when I read that first paragraph. It is so conclusive. Clarence wanted a vehicle that was faster, stronger, and more aggressive. The intentional Christian community strategy was completed, over and out. It had become barren. It was so yesteryear. Lonely, isolated, dusty, and occupied only by a few cobwebs of nostalgia, it sat like an abandoned shack on the riverbank of history. At least this was Clarence's verdict. It seems unjust.

---

1. Millard Fuller, *Bokotola* (Americus, GA: Habitat for Humanity International, 1977), 16.

The witness of Christian community, including Koinonia itself, produced fruit that should not be discounted. During the last half of the twentieth century there were a number of us growing up in southern evangelical circles who found our theology impotent, lacking the traction that would pull us out of the mudhole of silly doctrinal debates so we could begin to plow the fields of serious Christian discipleship. Our imagination sat on empty. We were separated from the life and ministry of Jesus by an ocean, a couple of continents, innumerable cultures, and 2,000 years of history. What could it possibly look like to take up the cross of Jesus or come together as the people of that first church who broke bread with glad and generous hearts and lived in a way that no one was in need?

We needed a new perspective; we needed an actual, live demonstration. "The goals and methods" of Koinonia, as articulated and designed by Clarence, provided that example for us. When we saw with the aid of his vision, when we witnessed the gospel enfleshed in Koinonia, the scales fell from our eyes. This twentieth century community of disciples was actually validated rather than discredited by its small size and struggles. Once we had ears, but we could not hear. Before the story of Koinonia we may have seen Jesus' mouth moving, but it sounded like Greek, or Aramaic, or Hebrew, who knows? We were confused. But when we heard Clarence's inspired recontextualization of the gospel, we understood. Jesus was not just calling us, he had chosen us. Just as Simon and Andrew dropped their nets and stepped out of their fishing boat, we were being asked to drop business as usual and step out of ordinariness to follow the living Lord.

A number of us who live in Christian community cannot talk about how we came to this without referring to Clarence. So I wish he had just softened that first paragraph a bit. If I had been a scribe sneaking around Koinonia the evening of October 20, 1968, I would have pulled out my X-Acto knife, intercepted this text, and made a small excision on the stencil before it got wrapped around the drum on the old mimeograph machine.

I'm not exaggerating the tension; the tone of this letter is very strong. Clarence talked about distancing himself geographically from Koinonia Farm, moving his family to Atlanta so he could be closer to an airport and take on the "communication" work of the new effort he called Partners. It also seemed, at least for a moment, that he envisioned a diminished role for Koinonia.[2]

---

2. Interestingly, in the version of the letter that currently appears on Koinonia Partners' website, Clarence called the emerging effort simply "Partners." However, lengthy

In retrospect, though, we know Clarence never repudiated intentional Christian community. He stayed at Koinonia for what turned out to be the last year of his life and deemed its platform the appropriate launching pad for Partners and the Fund for Humanity. Lenny Jordan, Clarence's son, wrote in a recent article in "Koinonia Farm Chronicle" that his father "always came back to the idea that . . . whatever direction he felt led by God, it would involve living in the way the early church lived—in intentional community."

Clarence's legacy in the intentional Christian community movement has never been called into question. Koinonia's very active commitment to keeping Clarence's flame alive and its reaffirmation in recent years of its identity as a community have further cemented the connection. Clarence didn't invent Christian communal living, but for many of us his name is synonymous with the practice of it in the United States.

Was Habitat Actually a Graft Rather than a Shoot?

As history would have it, I was not lurking in the shadows of the common building at Koinonia that fateful evening of 1968, and I did not profane what Clarence wrote. The Holy Spirit has a knack for taking the ingredients of sincerity and genuineness, sifting and stirring them with the deep emotions and yearnings of others, and cooking up a new culinary creation. As always, the proof of the pudding is in the eating. Clarence's strong and prophetic voice in the Fund for Humanity letter moved many people and eventually resulted in the 1976 birth of Habitat for Humanity and later in 2005 the Fuller Center for Housing. These Fund for Humanity progeny have survived and thrived, engaging literally millions of people as "partners" through volunteering and making financial donations. More than 500,000 of those partners are low-income families or individuals who have had their housing needs met.

For years the family resemblance between Koinonia and Habitat was unmistakable. In addition to Americus and a common history, they

---

excerpts of the letter used just a few years later by both Dallas Lee in *The Cotton Patch Evidence* (Americus, GA: Koinonia Partners, Inc., 1971) and Millard Fuller in *Bokotola* consistently use the name "Koinonia Partners." Koinonia continued to be community-based and had many characteristics of intentional Christian communities, but it does seem there was a clear change in its self-understanding after the 1968 letter. In 1976, on my first visit to Koinonia, one of the Partners, Al Zook, told me, "We are a Christian service organization, not a church-community."

shared stories, potluck meals, personnel, and a countercultural environment. Millard brought over from Koinonia several non-standard business practices—such as a needs-based salary structure—that looked like they had been designed by Jesus himself. In the early 1990s Millard pointed with pride to a *Non-Profit Times* article that cited Habitat as an extreme example of an organization with a sizable budget and inadequate financial reserves, with less than three days of operating funds in the bank. Yes, Habitat had multiple obligations including international partners serving around the world who were totally dependent on their monthly stipends. And, yes, in the spirit of Clarence, Habitat took seriously Jesus' exhortation to consider the lilies of the field and the birds of the air that were totally dependent on the providence of God.

Since conception Habitat has sought to grow—that was Clarence's and Millard's intention for the Fund for Humanity—and serious growth, not surprisingly, has brought change. Some of the changes are publicly visible (in recent years Habitat moved a substantial part of its headquarters to Atlanta and installed a second generation of senior leadership). Other changes are more internal and discernible only by those who are intimately involved in the organization, yet they are keenly felt.

As a result of these changes, the differences between Koinonia and Habitat as the best-known representatives of the two major branches of Clarence's family tree, intentional Christian community and Christian development organizations based on the Fund for Humanity vision, have become striking. One is small; one is large. One is intensely local; the other purposefully global. One has reclaimed its communal roots; the other is a corporation. One is intentionally countercultural; the other is very attentive to the value of its brand. One values simple living; the other seeks to stay competitive with similar not-for-profit salaries. One has reaffirmed itself as a community; the other has taken on a more sophisticated organizational structure and corporate culture along with an emphasis on performance measurement and evaluation, complex administrative systems, and professional communications.

There is no disavowal of each other and certainly no competition between the two. To the contrary, there remains a strong sense of mutual support and shared history. For example, Habitat's new Atlanta employees usually take a field trip to visit the Americus offices with a stopover for lunch at Koinonia. Nevertheless the differences are profound, obviously more than just a matter of appearance.

So on Clarence's 100th birthday the question begs to be asked (at least in my mind): do Habitat and Koinonia really share the same DNA? The respective nativity stories of the two groups are very well known, so it seems illogical to question parentage. But the dissimilarity is nagging. The one branch in terms of its sheer size dwarfs the rest of the tree, trunk and branches. Normal, organic growth can hardly explain the current state of reality. Is it possible that rather than Habitat being a native shoot out of the stump of Clarence, there was some sleight of hand, some subterfuge, someone else hiding out, maybe in the garden shed, who under the cover of night snuck out and grafted the Habitat branch on to the tree?

Another way of asking this same question is, has Habitat, which claims Clarence as a spiritual father, stayed true to his legacy through all of its growth and change? To verify, it's helpful to dig down to the tap root and examine that which defines Habitat's existence, our "Core Documents." How do our statements of vision, mission, and principles align in word and deed with those of Clarence?

Vision—A View of the "There"

Vision is a view of the "there." In theological language we could call it eschatology, or a theology of "the last things." Essentially, vision is a statement, a picture, a conviction, of what the heavens and the earth will look like when all is said and done, at the end of the day, in the fullness of time.

Not everyone or every organization has vision. Life can be lived without it, although human life is designed to be lived in the image of the divine and cannot be lived well without it. It is a given that any group emerging from the mind and labor of Clarence Jordan would have vision.

Dallas Lee's book, *The Substance of Faith and other Cotton Patch Sermons by Clarence Jordan*, published in 1972 just a few years after Clarence's death, closes with a short piece titled "A Spirit of Partnership." Clarence began with his own rendering of Joel 2:28–32.

> When the time is ripe, says God, I will shed my spirit on all mankind.
> And your sons and your daughters will speak truthfully.
> Your young people will come up with starry ideas,
> And your old people will have radical suggestions.
> Yes indeed, when the time is ripe I'll shed my spirit....

The shedding of God's spirit, Clarence explained, results in "a spirit of partnership. The rich man will sit down at the same table with a poor man and learn how good cornbread and collard greens are, and the poor man will find out what a T-bone steak tastes like. Neither will shiver in a drafty house, nor have to move furniture when it rains."[3]

In his own beautiful prose with a gift of illuminating the universal with the local, Clarence described a peaceable community, a place where everyone had enough and no one had too much, where there was no prejudice, and where the practice of humility and generosity were the common currency. Then he went global, "God's spirit will call the people from the East to join hands with the people from the West, and the people from the North to join hands with the people from the South and all will seek the other's good. None will smite his brothers, nor deal deceitfully. They will sing at their labors, and be thankful for the fruits of the fields and factories."

A couple of paragraphs later Clarence escaped gravity itself with a celestial conclusion.

"God's spirit will give eyes to mankind with which to see the glory of the Lord. God's spirit will give ears to mankind to hear the sound of his trumpet as well as his still small voice. He will dwell with us and be our God, and we shall be his people. He will wipe away our tears, dispel our doubt, remove our fears, and lead us out. He will heal the brokenhearted, open the eyes of the blind, release the captives, preach the good news to the poor, and usher in the acceptable year of the Lord. He will bulldoze the mountains and fill in the valleys, he will make the rough places smooth and the crooked ways straight."

In this short piece Clarence drew from the vision of Jesus, from the prophets, from Peter, and from John of Patmos. It is magnificent and breathtaking, and it brings tears to my eyes each time I read it. Clarence had a view of the there. The man had vision. In the introduction to his book, Dallas Lee wrote that "The Spirit of Partnership" reflected "the vision that burned in Clarence most of his life. Koinonia Partners grew out of that vision and seeks today to give it expression through a Fund for Humanity . . ."

One biblical theme often used to explain the vision of economic leveling and abundance is jubilee, recorded in Leviticus 25, a practice given by God to the Israelites. In the sabbath year, every seventh year, the Israelites were to reaffirm their dependence on God in a very tangible fashion by letting their land lie fallow. In the jubilee year, the fiftieth year at the end of seven cycles of sabbath years, the ante was upped with the forgiveness of

---

3. Clarence Jordan, *The Substance of Faith and Other Cotton Patch Sermons*, ed. Dallas Lee (Eugene, OR: Cascade, 2005).

debts, the release of slaves and captives, and the redistribution of capital by the return of property to tribal families. The blast from the horn of jubilee called for a massive, radical adjustment, a releveling so that society could be released from the bonds of its accumulated injustices and the community could escape from the dead end of sin that had resulted in poverty, oppression, and despair for many. Jubilee was dependent upon the spirit of God; it reaffirmed the spirit of partnership among the people of Israel. The people of Israel were not healthy and whole until all were healthy and whole.

It is possible, as Jesus stood in the synagogue of his hometown Nazareth and read from the scroll of Isaiah, he was not just calling upon the jubilee tradition, but actually announcing the year of jubilee.

> The Spirit of the Lord is upon me,
> because he has anointed me to bring good news to the poor.
> He has sent me to proclaim release to the captives
> and recovery of sight to the blind,
> to let the oppressed go free,
> to proclaim the year of the Lord's favor.
> (Luke 4:18–19)

This passage was for Clarence the foundation of the Fund for Humanity. He quoted it often, including it both in his 1968 letter and in "The Spirit of Partnership."

In 1981, when Habitat for Humanity was five years old and still relatively small, Millard, quizzed by an interviewer on a radio show about how many houses Habitat would build, responded, "Our goal is to eliminate poverty housing from the face of the earth." With this backdrop of the jubilee and Jesus traditions appropriated by Clarence, Millard as a faithful messenger and organizational engineer of the Fund for Humanity vision could not have said anything less. We'll keep building, in other words, until everyone, everywhere has a decent place to live, and it will happen.

"A decent place to live" for Habitat for Humanity has always meant more than house construction. It includes good neighborhoods, good relationships, and all other related aspects of individual and collective well-being. For Habitat, "a decent place to live" is both an element of and a metaphor for the peaceable community.

Over time, Millard's 1981 statement about our goal has been framed organizationally as Habitat's vision statement. It now reads simply, "A world where everyone has a decent place to live." The words are not as poetic or as soaring as the passage from Joel, but it contains the essentials of Clarence's vision. It is global, meaning everywhere ("a world where"). It is universal, meaning it benefits all ("everyone has"). And it is prophetic, meaning it calls for comprehensive transformation ("a decent place to live").

Mission—From Here to There

Mission has to do with what we do. If the "there" of the vision was already fully realized, then it would be here, and there would be no need for vision. We know, though, Clarence's spirit of partnership is a vision, for currently the poor are still poor and the rich are yet rich, and they are not sitting at the same table eating collard greens and steak. Many do not sing at their labors for they have no work; the mountains have yet to be bulldozed and the valleys yet to be filled; and a large part of the world's population lives in places that are not decent. Mission is what we do in response.

Theoretically a theory of change should be able to draw a solid line from what we do to the "there." In other words, a theory of change will explain how the work of our mission will bring about the reality of the vision. "Theoretically" is key, because the connection between our labor and the outcome is always problematic. Most religious visions and many not-for-profit ones are to a large degree global, universal, and prophetic. The closer these visions come to the eschaton (the completion of all things, divinely orchestrated if not ordained), the more difficult it becomes to presume, predict, or pretend that the outcome will be produced by our action. Nevertheless, our work must have some connection to the end goal; it should reflect the vision and contribute to it, even if it falls far short of achieving it.

Clarence said in the 1968 letter that he found the change theory of intentional Christian community to be inadequate, that is, "too slow, too weak, and not aggressive" enough. The destination, namely the realm of God, was the same, but to move in that direction a new "vehicle" was needed, one that would be quicker, stronger, and more proactive.

It was more complicated, though, than just trading in the old mare for a thoroughbred racehorse. Clarence posited three needs for the new effort.

1. *Adaptability*. Clarence actually called it mobility. He was very concerned about changes in the economy and in agriculture that were leading to the displacement of sharecropper, tenant, and small farmers. He may have feared that Koinonia would end up with no neighbors. Intentional community was standing flat-footed; by definition it was stationary, unable to

embrace new programs while the environment, in this case the agricultural economy, was undergoing a radical change. The God Movement, as Clarence called the realm of God (after all, this was the 1960s), existed in the world and needed to adapt its agenda in response to changes rapidly happening in the world.

2. *A comprehensive, proactive program.* Clarence outlined plans for three initiatives: communication, instruction, and application. Communication entailed public relations and education, recruitment, and consciousness-raising, i.e., spreading the vision far and wide. It was to carry on this specific work that Clarence imagined himself moving to Atlanta. Instruction involved the education of individuals in skills and values for living out the vision. Instruction was needed for everyone, not just the poor. The affluent would have to learn how to live generously in partnership, divesting themselves of their abundance in an honest and just manner. Application was the implementation of the vision in the new, alternative economic structure called the Fund for Humanity. The Fund in turn would have three program initiatives:

   a. Partnership Agriculture—making land available for poor people to farm.
   b. Partnership Industries—business development, essentially training and capitalization for the establishment of micro-enterprises for those who needed jobs.
   c. Partnership Housing—development of affordable housing solutions specifically in rural areas for the low-income.

3. *Large scale and growing engagement.* This was not going to be a small effort. Everyone needed to be involved for the vision called for universal, systemic, and spiritual change. Clarence saw greed as causative and symptomatic of sin and economic injustice. Sin was humanity's spiritual alienation from God, the lack of belief in God's beneficence and love, and the unwillingness of people to trust in God's provision. Economic injustice was the practical manifestation of sin when those who have the world's goods hoard, accumulate, and build bigger barns.

The consequence was a fractured world, disparity within the human community, and division between God and humans. As an answer to the deficit created by sin, the Fund for Humanity called for

- spiritual investment through its challenge to everyone, affluent and poor, to be generous and share with each other;
- economic investment with the provision of capital for the low-income; and
- collective or communal wealth building through a land trust mechanism and an ever-increasing capital fund built through donations and loan repayments.

The fund in Clarence's words would be "self-generative and ever expanding." He expected a profound change in the economic and spiritual life of humanity. It is in this expectation of growth that Clarence's theory of change is clearly visible. The scale of the new effort was to be determined not by the financial need of the poor, but by the size of the world's population. Fulfillment was not going to be delivered by ramped up production that would eliminate need, i.e., x number of cooperative farms established, y number of jobs, or z number of houses built so that the need of the poor was eliminated. The theory of change had to do with engagement or involvement. Both rich and poor had needs. The poor "need capital," while the rich "need a wise, honorable and just way of divesting themselves of their over-abundance." For Clarence divestment had not just extrinsic value so the poor would have more, it had intrinsic value for it was the antidote to greed. He closed his 1968 letter with a quote from St. Augustine and a very strong challenge to the affluent: "He who possesses a surplus possesses the goods of others." That's a polite way of saying that anybody who has too much is a thief. If you are a "thief," perhaps you should set a reasonable living standard for your family and restore the "stolen goods" to humanity, either through the Fund or by some other suitable means.

Ultimate Change Would Happen When Everyone Fulfilled Their Role as Partners

Habitat for Humanity's mission statement aligns well with Clarence's and Millard's intention for the Fund for Humanity. It reads: "Seeking to put God's love into action, Habitat for Humanity brings people together to build homes, communities and hope." The statement sets God's providence as the context, calls for public engagement as the methodology, and identifies end products or benefits that are elemental (homes), social (communities), and spiritual (hope). Habitat for Humanity in its execution of the mission over the last thirty-six years has fulfilled Clarence's and Millard's desire for a vehicle that is adaptable (or responsive to changes in the environment), comprehensive, and proactive in its educational, public relations, and operations, and reaches for scale in its engagement of large numbers of people.

Contained in Habitat's mission statement is a theory of change that is largely consistent with Clarence. Millard hoped Habitat would "become the conscience of the world in the matter of housing," so he wanted to see everyone involved, "the whole crowd"; poverty housing would be eliminated when it became religiously, politically, and socially unacceptable. It is actually this strategy of engagement rather than reduction of construction cost that is at the root of Habitat's use of volunteers. This is visible in Habitat for Humanity's 2014–2018 strategic plan.

Habitat's scaling approach focuses on facilitating improvements for a sufficient number of households, in a sufficient number of communities, to help the public understand the need and potential for community change. This in turn drives: a) broader engagement in housing solutions; b) support for market development; and c) demand for policies and systems that create new opportunities for those in need of adequate, affordable shelter.

"Largely consistent" is qualified, which means there is not a perfect overlay of the two theories of change. Habitat does bank on public engagement, but its strategy does not include the frontal assault on greed that was so characteristic of Clarence, an issue that is acknowledged in the last section of this essay.

Principles and Collard Greens

Principles are the rubber bumpers that keep our mission efforts aimed toward the vision. Without principles, our passions, neuroses, delusions, and fears will spin us straight into the gutters of accommodation or exploitation of others. Principles are the external reference points that provide perspective so we will know where we are and where we are headed; they are the satellite behind our moral and visional GPS. Without principles we end up in a roadless wilderness, denuded of our integrity, clothed only by a sheer, thin pragmatism.

Prophets eat principles for dinner, along with their collard greens. Both are good sources of iron and fortitude, providing the strength to publicly advocate a diet currently deemed unpalatable by society. It was not easy for Clarence to be a pacifist during World War II. And his commitment to being an outspoken egalitarian on issues of race and class in the deep South during the 1940s and 1950s was costly, not only putting Koinonia in danger but, no doubt, sacrificing its ability to achieve other important objectives.

A principled person often is greatly admired by others, but admiration is an empty reward if the crowd doesn't like collard greens, that is, if people keep their distance because the standards are perceived as too heroic or the lifestyle as too high of a price to pay. Very principled people may also be dismissed—by the judgment of others or even by their own self-judgment—as irrelevant, iconoclastic, or naive. The first paragraph of Clarence's letter reads to me as though he was struggling with these judgments.

I do suspect, though, that Clarence's staying at Koinonia was not only the rebound of his conviction that shared, communal life was the most efficacious setting for Christian discipleship and ministry, but was also from a renewed sense that it would provide a compelling demonstration of the vision. Even though we may not live in a community of goods, we are better prepared to anticipate and join the messianic banquet of Matthew 22 because of the visible picture we are given in Acts 2 of the Jerusalem community gathered around the common table, breaking bread with glad and generous hearts. In the same way, with the shared life of Koinonia as the launching pad, Clarence's audience for the Fund for Humanity was more inclined to commit itself to personal sacrifice so that no one should be in need. His vision would have to some degree been diminished if he had left the community of Koinonia to take up residence near the Atlanta airport.

Habitat for Humanity was still young when it began to shed Koinonia culture. Maintaining the needs-based salary structure ended up requiring meetings upon meetings to develop complex rules, negotiate lifestyles, and determine exceptions; it was gone by the early 1980s. Eventually the organization realized that subsistence salaries or stipends, when not supported by a community of goods, resulted in an employee base that would be either: a) limited to those who were already supported by some external source of income such as an employed spouse or independent wealth or b) would include many who would themselves be in need of a Habitat house. Neither of these conclusions—a lack of diversity or a non-livable wage scale—were acceptable for an organization that advocates for a more just society. It is not right to conclude that these developments represent an abandonment of foundational principles; Habitat was not designed to be an intentional Christian community. Even the move to Atlanta that Clarence himself did not undertake seems inevitable in Habitat history when growth was necessary in order to achieve its founding intent.

Habitat for Humanity has, however, kept its orientation with a commitment to the principles of the Fund for Humanity. Following are Habitat's five mission principles. I've excerpted a few phrases from each principle and then added a parallel quote from Clarence's 1968 letter.

1. Demonstrate the love of Jesus Christ. "We undertake our work to demonstrate the love and teachings of Jesus, acting in all ways in accord with the belief that God's love and grace abound for all . . ."

Clarence: "By communication we mean the sowing of the seed, the spreading of the radical ideas of the gospel message; the call to faith in God and the reshaping and restructuring of our lives around his will and purpose . . ."

2. Focus on shelter. "We have chosen, as our means of manifesting God's love, to create opportunities for all people to live in decent, durable shelter."

Clarence: "But how can these things become flesh and blood? How does the dream become deed and the vision reality? Can the lofty speculation be transformed into practical, hard-nosed action?"

3. Advocate for affordable housing. "And, in all of our work, we will seek to put shelter on hearts and minds in such powerful ways that poverty housing becomes socially, politically, and religiously unacceptable."

Clarence: "Communication . . . means to 'preach good news to the poor, to proclaim release to the captives and recovering of sight to the blind, to set at liberty those who are oppressed, to proclaim the acceptable year of the Lord.' To do this we will use every available means of modern communication."

4. Promote dignity and hope. We believe that every person has something to contribute and something to gain from creating communities in which all people have decent, affordable places to live.

Clarence: "Out of gratitude for what others have done to set [a person] free, he should himself share generously and cheerfully to help set others free. Or as Jesus put it, 'You have received it as a gift, so share it as a gift.'"

5. Support sustainable and transformational development. "We view our work as successful when it transforms lives and promotes positive and lasting social, economic and spiritual change within a community."

Clarence: "So we want to throw every ounce of our weight into helping men to radically restructure their lives so as to be in partnership with God."

Working within the parameters of these principles is not easy, nor should we expect it would be. Critics, the inevitable dynamics of organizational growth, changes in the economy, and even stakeholders often are pushing or pulling Habitat to move beyond these principles. The temptation to sacrifice them may appear in the guise of relevance, urgency, inclusiveness, destiny, opportunity, or self-preservation.

The Spirit of Clarence

I'm convinced that Habitat for Humanity's core documents are Jordanian, through and through, and, as someone who resides on the inside of Habitat, I'm confident they are authoritative. I've heard Habitat International's senior leaders adamantly defend them and state they are non-negotiable.

We have acknowledged it is not easy for an organization seeking to be "fast, strong, and aggressive" in the fulfillment of its mission to stay true to its Christian identity. Our new strategic planning document is prefaced by a prayer that emerged from a year-long conversation, involving hundreds of Habitat stakeholders from around the globe, about what is most important to this ministry. It reads:

> God teach us humility so that we may listen,
> confess and forgive,
> serve in relationship with the poor,
> persevere in our mission,
> unify as one body with many diverse parts,
> and act with courage and boldness.

For a large, global organization whose "brand" value is now estimated in billions of dollars, it is radical to begin a five-year plan with a petition for humility and an aspiration to listen, confess, and forgive. As a shoot from the stump of Clarence, a man who struggled with how vision, mission, and principles interface with effectiveness and strategy, it would be naive for us to think we should be exempt from the same.

Mechanistically aligning our organizational documents with a foundational letter penned by Clarence is ultimately not the point. Clarence was a man of spirit. The stories of Clarence, his writings, and even his legacy remind me of the ethics of Jesus and of his ecclesiology (how we organize our collective life as God's people). His primary Christ-likeness, though, was in his desire for, expectation of, and sensitivity to the movement of

God's spirit in the world. Joel's prophecy of the shedding of God's spirit on all of humanity was Clarence's hope. The founding of the Fund for Humanity was precipitated by his own "spiritual vacuum" and Millard's "spiritual crisis." The vision was attributed to a "leading of God's spirit," and would result in a "new spirit of partnership." The word *spirit* or *spiritual* was used eleven times in the four pages of the 1968 letter.

"A shoot shall come out from the stump of Jesse," the prophet Isaiah wrote of the messiah, "and a branch shall grow out of his roots. The spirit of the Lord shall rest on him, the spirit of wisdom and understanding, the spirit of counsel and might, the spirit of knowledge and the fear of the Lord." As a follower of Jesus, Clarence also was imbued with the spirit of the Lord. Millard was fond of saying, "Habitat for Humanity is a movement of the Holy Spirit in our time." The most important test for being in the spirit of Clarence, and this is my opinion, not official Habitat dictum, comes down to matters of the spirit.

I would posit three such issues that are implicit, not explicit, in Habitat's values, and present for us both profound opportunities and, at times, vexing challenges as we seek to experience, contribute to, and reach for spiritual and social redemption (otherwise known as transformation).

1. *A spirit of wisdom and understanding.* The challenge: to be attuned to the spirit of God. Clarence at the end of his letter wrote to the friends of Koinonia, "I beg you to pray that we may have the wisdom, humility, patience and love to be faithful to him who has called us to this exciting venture." We, Habitat for Humanity, have learned a lot from the world, as we should, about leadership, management, planning, and performance. There are times, however, when those in the spirit of God are called and led to take directions that may not appear to be strategic or profitable or to invest in efforts that may not meet accepted standards of measurability or reasonability. Witness Jesus, who turned his face, at a supposedly inopportune moment, to go to Jerusalem and his crucifixion, or witness Clarence, who knew when to go to southwest Georgia, when to call for the Fund for Humanity, and when to stay in Americus.

There are many voices speaking to Habitat that claim they can provide the wisdom and understanding necessary for success, but there is only one that will lead us to the promised land where everyone has a decent place to live. The challenge for a multinational corporation, whose stakeholders number in at least the tens of thousands, to listen and then articulate the leading of God's spirit, is daunting. The alternative, though, is to abnegate our hope of participating in God's ultimate work of transformation.

It is difficult, by definition, to state this particular challenge in a specific way or to make it concrete, for, as Jesus said, "The wind blows where it chooses, and you hear the sound of it, but you do not know where it comes from or where it goes. So it is with everyone who is born of the Spirit" (John 3:8). It takes constant vigilance and attentiveness. Perhaps a good way to approach this, figuratively speaking, would be to stop and have a prayer meeting every time we utter the word *strategy* or *measurement*. Habitat is actually doing this, so to speak, by having a task force dedicated to "keeping God at the center" in the context of its current five-year strategic planning process.

2. *A spirit of counsel and might.* The challenge: to be prophetic. Clarence's formula was two-sided, "What the poor need is not charity but capital, not case-workers, but co-workers. And what the rich need is a wise, honorable and just way of divesting themselves of their over-abundance." The biblical message is clear: in the fullness of God's realm, when we gather around the banquet table, there will be many kinds of diversity with one notable exception, there will no rich and poor. Each one who has a stool will have a glad and generous heart; all will be ready to share everything they have. Clarence's invitation called for divesting as well as investing. Divestiture was not simply a means to the end of providing charity; it was a frontal assault on greed. Those who cling to what they have, who find security, ego-satisfaction, or whatever in having too much, are declining the invitation. "Sell your possessions," Jesus commanded. "Make purses for yourselves that do not wear out . . . For where your treasure is, there your heart will be also" (Luke 12:33–34).

In the first half of Habitat's life this challenge was articulated regularly. "If you've got two houses, give one away," Millard would preach. In the second half, as the organization worked harder and harder to raise more money, long before the change in senior leadership, this exhortation fell by the wayside. It is not effective fundraising to challenge the lifestyle of the wealthy who are paying the bills and providing the charity. Moreover, as Habitat became more successful and better-known, and with changes in the philanthropic environment in the United States, the organization has shifted its resource development emphasis from individual donations to institutional giving to government funds to earned income. This progression is not wrong in and of itself, but it has contributed to the unfortunate result that the invitation to the affluent—to pull up a stool and join the party, to be radically generous and glad—is less clear and compelling.

3. *Spirit of knowledge and fear of the Lord.* The challenge: to sing at our labor. "It is extremely doubtful that with all our knowledge and skill we will be any more successful in saving ourselves than were the men of old," Clarence wrote, comparing contemporary efforts to cure society's ills with the story of the people of Babel who attempted to "build a city and a tower with its top in the heavens" (Gen 11). With his great vision and his spirit of activism, Clarence must have understood this temptation—to save ourselves—in a very personal way. He knew, however, that without a correct sense of priorities in our approach to the transcendent and the temporal, we will find ourselves in a barren and desolate place, grimly and desperately laboring, until we are crushed by the futility of our own efforts.

The Fund for Humanity's first and foremost objective was not to build a more just society, but instead to help people "radically restructure their lives so as to be in partnership with God." In Scripture this type of partnership is often called "the fear of the Lord," that respectful relationship in which we accept our role as junior partners to God's senior status, allowing God to remain in charge of design and ultimate fulfillment. If "partnership with God" could be characterized as the vertical relationship, then the lateral is "a new spirit—a spirit of partnership with one another," or human society. The vertical is empty and meaningless without the lateral, nobody preached that more than Clarence, but the lateral was impossible without the vertical. This was the knowledge Clarence had; Isaiah's summary was, "The fear of the Lord is Zion's treasure" (33:6). When this partnership is regained, human beings will let loose of their fear—and "sing at their labor," as Clarence described in "The Spirit of Partnership."

To stay in the spirit of Clarence, or even more importantly in the spirit of knowledge and fear of the Lord, I wish we could rein in our use of the word *urgency*. The fact of 1.6 billion people living in substandard housing around the globe is shocking, tragic, shameful, unacceptable, and urgent. However, it is not spiritually or humanly sustainable for us as an organization to work with a sense of urgency, in an adrenalin-fueled state, day after day, year after year, decade after decade. When we are urgent, we must get "it" done immediately; we will stay up all night, forget all other priorities, break rules, and abandon principles with little forethought. And at some point we will collapse in a heap. I suggest that when we describe the situation as "urgent," we then proceed to use an alternative word such as *passionate* to describe our work. Passion acknowledges both that we suffer (compassion—to suffer with) as long as even one does not have decent housing and that we have joy in our confidence God will deliver the vision, a world where everyone has a decent place to live.

All of these tensions for Habitat for Humanity are inherent in Clarence's ambition for a vehicle that would be faster, stronger, and more aggressive. Perhaps, and this could be a discussion for philosophers, theologians, and social theorists, there was (or is) an internal contradiction in Clarence with his global vision and mission on the one hand and his prophetic principles and countercultural style on the other. If so, Clarence kept good company, because the same could be said of Jesus. May Habitat continue in this same spirit.

A Personal Letter from Clarence Jordan to Friends of Koinonia

October 21, 1968

For several years it has been clear that Koinonia stands at the end of an era or perhaps its existence. Its goals and methods which were logical and effective in the 1940's and 50's seem no longer relative to an age which is undergoing vast and rapid changes. An integrated, Christian community was a very practical vehicle through which to bear witness to a segregated society a decade ago, but now it is too slow, too weak, not aggressive enough. Its lack of mobility gives it the appearance of a house on the bank of a river as the rushing torrents of history swirl by, leaving it with but memories of its active past. Other factors, which cannot be mentioned here, also contributed to the feeling that this approach is no longer valid.

One, however, must be mentioned, and that is the agricultural situation. When Koinonia was begun in 1942, farming in the South was still somewhat simple and there was great need and opportunity for the skills which we were able to contribute to the situation. During those 10 to 15 years we had considerable impact upon the agricultural problems of this area. But in recent years the big machines and the business experts have swept the sharecroppers, tenants and little farmers off the land and into the ghetto. And we feel as needed and as effective as a freezer display at an Eskimo convention.

Something had to give. The obvious answer was to call it quits. The group had already dwindled, for a variety of reasons, to a mere handful— two families, to be exact. About a year ago, Florence and I decided that we would seek other directions for our lives. Warm and loyal friends extended us invitations to join faculties, to pastor churches, to be this-and-that-in-residence, etc. Some of these were challenging; one I had just about decided to accept. But somehow, nothing seemed to really click. Perhaps I was suffering from "battle fatigue" or was just plain tired. For quite a while it was as though I were living in a spiritual vacuum. No joy, no excitement, no sense of mission.

In this state of torpor, I got a very brief note from Millard Fuller, director of the Tougaloo College Development Committee. My first contact with Millard was in December of 1965 when he came by here to visit for a half-hour with his friend Al Henry, who was living here at the time. Millard was then about 30, a tremendously successful business man and outstanding layman in the United Church of Christ. As the half-hour stretched into a day and the day finally into a month, we learned that this was a time of deep spiritual crisis for Millard and his wife, Linda, and that both had reached the brink of destruction. Millard had become "a money addict" and was more enslaved to it than any alcoholic to his bottle. So great was his appetite that he had already become a millionaire and was reaching for more. But God reached for him, turned him around, and gave him the wisdom to do what even the rich young ruler in the bible wouldn't do—"Go, sell what thou hast and give it to the poor, and come, follow me." During that month here he transacted by phone much of the business necessary by liquidating his assets in Montgomery, Alabama, and distributing them to charitable purposes. Being a white native of Alabama, Millard wanted to express his discipleship to Christ in selfless service to blacks. He got a job raising money for Tougaloo College, a Negro school near Jackson, Mississippi. In this, he was both happy and successful.

His note to me in May of this year was brief and direct. "I have just resigned my job with Tougaloo. What have you got up your sleeve?" Nothing. Nothing up my sleeve or in my head or heart. I'm blank. But wait a minute. Does God have something up his sleeve—for both of us? I got on the phone and called Millard at his New York office. Could God be trying to say something to us, to accomplish some purpose through us?

We decided to get together at once and discuss it. I would be preaching in a few days at the Oakhurst Baptist Church in Atlanta. Millard said he should fly down and meet me there. The pastor of the church, John Nichol, turned his study over to us and we spent all day talking and praying. At the end, both of us were convinced that God had given a radically new direction to our lives.

We still cannot fully articulate this leading of God's Spirit. But we had the deep feeling that modern man's problems stem almost entirely from his loss of any sense of meaningful participation with God in His purposes for mankind. For most people God really and truly is dead, stone dead. Or perhaps he has never been alive. With no upward reach, with no sense of partnership with God, man has chosen to be a loner, trying to solve on his own, but always in deep frustration and desperation, crushing problems which increasingly threaten to destroy him. Like the ancient architects of Babel, he proudly and

A Personal Letter from Clarence Jordan to Friends of Koinonia

pitifully calls, "Come, let us build ourselves a city, and a tower with its top in the heavens, and let us make a name for ourselves, lest we be scattered abroad upon the face of the whole earth." And it is extremely doubtful that with all our knowledge and skill we will be any more successful in saving ourselves than were the men of old. From bitter experience we should know by now that "unless the Lord builds the house, those who build it labor in vain. Unless the Lord watches over the city, the watchman stays awake in vain."

The church has been saying this all along, but has not believed its own message. So it has thrown up its hands and joined the multitudes who look to the Government for salvation. But even with billions of dollars at its disposal, Government cannot give man a God-dimension to his life. It is inherently incapable of reaching the inner recesses of man's being, which must be touched if life on this planet is to be even passingly tolerable.

So we want to throw every ounce of our weight into helping men to radically restructure their lives so as to be in partnership with God. Later I'll give more specific details about how we will go about this.

It has also become clear to us that as man has lost his identity with God he has lost it with his fellow man. We fiercely compete with one another as if we were enemies, not brothers. We want only to kill human beings for whom Christ died. Our cities provide us anonymity, not community. Instead of partners, we are aliens and strangers. Greed consumes us, and self-interest separates us and confines us to ourselves or our own group.

As a result, the poor are being driven from rural areas; hungry, frustrated, angry masses are huddled in the cities; suburbanites walk in fear; the chasm between blacks and whites grows wider and deeper; war hysteria invades every nook and cranny of the earth.

We must have a new spirit—a spirit of partnership with one another.

But how can these things become flesh and blood? How does the dream become deed and the vision reality? Can the lofty speculation be transformed into practical, hard-nosed action?

Even though both Millard and I are dreamers and visionaries, we have had plenty of experience with the stern, down-to-earth facts of life. Yet these questions overwhelmed us, and we desperately felt the need to share the vision with and seek the counsel of spiritually sensitive men of God. Accordingly, we called together in mid-August about fifteen such men to come to Koinonia for a four-day session of seeking, thinking, talking. They were business men, politicians, writers, ministers, free-lancers—all with a deep compassion for their fellow man. From this conference emerged a course of action which, for want of a better word, we shall call PARTNERS. It has three prongs: 1) Communication; 2) Instruction; 3) Application.

1) By communication we mean the sowing of the seed, the spreading of the radical ideas of the gospel message; the call to faith in God and the reshaping and restructuring of our lives around his will and purpose; the promise of a new spirit which produces a new way of life. It means "to preach good news to the poor, to proclaim release to the captives and recovering of sight to the blind, to set at liberty those who are oppressed, to proclaim the acceptable year of the Lord." To do this we will use every available means of modern communication. We will travel and speak extensively across the land and throughout the world. We will make tapes, records, films, publish books and circulate literature in every way possible. Already a good start has been made in this direction, but it will greatly intensified.

It was felt that I should get to work on this immediately, and that Millard should assume full responsibility for the administration of Koinonia so that I can be released as soon as possible. The transfer should be complete by the first of the year, when my family will move somewhere into the Atlanta area. Being near a large airport will greatly facilitate travel, and the opportunities for "communication" will be much better in this great cross-roads of the South.

2) By instruction we mean the constant teaching and training of the "partners" to enable them to become more effective and mature. There will be traveling "schools" to follow up and conserve the results of the speaking and communicating, to keep alive the new spirit, to strengthen and encourage. The first such school is already scheduled for early January. There will also be conferences and retreats, such as one held here at Koinonia, October 18-20. Some of the present facilities here will no doubt be used increasingly for this purpose.

3) Application, in its initial stages, will consist of partnership industries, partnership farming, and partnership housing. These will be implemented through a FUND FOR HUMANITY.

The FUND has already been set up and is being incorporated as a non-profit organization. Its purpose will be two-fold: a) to provide an inheritance for the disinherited, and b) to provide a means through which the possessed may share with and invest in the dispossessed. What the poor need is not charity but capital, not case-workers, but co-workers. And what the rich need is a wise, honorable and just way of divesting themselves of their over-abundance. The Fund for Humanity will meet both of these needs.

A Personal Letter from Clarence Jordan to Friends of Koinonia

Money for the Fund will come from shared gifts by those who feel that they have more than they need, from non-interest bearing loans from those who cannot afford to make the gift but who do want to provide working capital for the disinherited, and from the voluntarily shared profits from the partnership industries, farms and houses. As a starter, it has been agreed to transfer all of Koinonia Farm's assets of about $250,000 to the Fund. Other gifts are already beginning to come in.

The Fund will give away no money. It is not a hand-out. It will provide capital for the partnership enterprises.

The first enterprise to be launched is partnership farming. Under this plan all land will be held in trust by the Fund for Humanity but will be used by the partners free of charge. Thus, usership will replace ownership. This can be done because the Fund's capital has been provided by those who care and there is no need to pay interest on it. This is extremely important, for under the present system a farmer with an investment of $150,000, which is not at all unusual, will pay $10,500 a year in interest alone when figured at 7%. (We know farmers who are paying 8%.) Thus, with corn at the present price of about $1 a bushel and the profit at about 30¢, the farmer would have to produce 35,000 bushels just to pay his interest. He simply can't bear this crushing load. He can either quit, move to the city and go on relief, or he must inherit the land—from his earthly father or his Heavenly Father. A poor man's hope lies only in the latter.

The Fund for Humanity seeks to provide such an inheritance. And like all inheritances, a man does not pay rent or interest on it. But out of gratitude for what others have done to set him free, he should himself share generously and cheerfully to help set others free. Or as Jesus put it, "You have received it as a gift, so share it as a gift." The partners, then, will be strongly encouraged, though not required, to contribute at liberally as possible to the Fund so as to keep enlarging it and making more capital available to others. If the partners have the right spirit (and I cannot see how this or any system can work without that) and there should be growing numbers—which it seems reasonable to predict—the Fund should be self-generative and ever expanding.

We think that each partnership unit should consist of one to four partners, with the units grouped close enough to cooperate with machinery, labor, and social, recreational and spiritual activities.

In addition to capital, the partners may need technical advice and spiritual nurture. These experts and shepherds will be provided by the PARTNERS organization. We anticipate that there will be volunteers arising from the speaking and teaching activities.

We have here over 1,000 acres with which to begin now. The Wittkampers will continue here as a partner family, and another family—the Al Zooks—have already arrived. Al and Ann have four young children, and while coming here directly from Reba Place Fellowship in Evanston, IL, they have had much farm experience. A local Negro family is very "warm" and will possibly become the Zooks's partners, sharing equally with them in the enterprise. Some high school boys, who want to earn college money, will probably set up a cattle feeding operation. (One young "partner" experimented along this line this year and did quite well.) In each instance, land and capital are provided but not given, on faith, at no charge. As the partners are able, they will repay the capital over and above their gifts to the Fund, so as to free it to be invested elsewhere. The land remains in permanent trust and is therefore freed from the evils of speculation.

The same principles will be applied to partnership industries. We already have a fairly flourishing pecan shelling plant, fruit cake bakery, candy kitchen and mail order business. Once again, partners will operate these ventures with no capital outlay in the beginning and never any rent or interest. Here again PARTNERS will provide technical assistance and pastoral care in its finest sense. As the businesses become successful, they should free the original capital and also enlarge the Fund for Humanity to foster other undertakings in needy areas both here and in other lands. Millard Fuller is an extremely imaginative, energetic, and practical business man (he had to be to make his million in a mere eight years) and already has some brilliant ideas for other partnership industries.

Partnership housing is concerned with the idea that the urban ghetto is to a considerable extent the product of rural displacement. People don't move to the city unless life in the country has become intolerable or impossible. They do not voluntarily choose the degrading life in the big city slums; it is forced upon them. If the land in the country is made available to them on which to build a decent house, and if they can get jobs nearby to support their families, they'll stay put.

So we have recently laid off 42 half-acre home sites and are making them available to displaced rural families. Four acres in the center are being reserved as a community park and recreational are. Twenty of the tracts are being sold outright for a nominal sum and the families will make their own arrangements for building and financing. The other 22 sites will be developed according to partnership principles. The Fund for Humanity will put up a four-bedroom house with bath, kitchen and living room (this can be done at

A Personal Letter from Clarence Jordan to Friends of Koinonia

present costs for $5500, lot and all), and this will be sold to a family over a 20-year period with no interest, only a small monthly administration charge. Thus the cost will be about $25 a month as compared with $57 a month for the usual interest-bearing financing. For a poor person, this can be the difference between owning a house and not owning one. The interest forces him to pay for two but get only one.

As with farming and industries, the partner family will gradually free the initial capital to build houses for others, and will be encouraged to share at least a part of their savings on interest with the Fund for Humanity. Even as all are benefited, so should all share. If, as Jesus says, "It is more blessed to give than to get," then even the poorest should not be denied the extra blessedness of giving.

Perhaps I have now given you at least some understanding of PARTNERS and the new direction for my own life. I would like to encourage each of you to rethink your life and make whatever adjustments you feel necessary to bring it into line with the will of God. Augustine once said, "He who possesses a surplus possesses the goods of others." That's a polite way of saying that anybody who has too much is a thief. If you are a "thief," perhaps you should set a reasonable living standard for your family and restore the "stolen goods" to humanity, either through the Fund or by some other suitable means. Some of you may wish to join us and seek the new life or partnership with God and man. Above all, I beg you to pray that we may have the wisdom, humility, patience and love to be faithful to him who has called us to this exciting venture. And may God's peace rule in your hearts.

Yours in faith and expectation,

Clarence Jordan

Afterword

"*Feed the hungry.*" It seemed clear this was what we were called to do as we set out to return to the original vision for Koinonia Farm. Feed the hungry physically by learning to naturally grow and distribute healthy food. Feed the hungry spiritually by continuing to offer hospitality, by conducting an internship several times a year, giving talks, teaching classes, keeping Clarence Jordan's books in print, maybe even by organizing a symposium.

We at Koinonia Farm believe the Clarence Jordan Symposium is one of the fruits born from the return to the communal roots.

For us, farming is both a root and a fruit of our life together. Wayne Weiseman delivers in "Koinonia Farm and the Permaculture Movement" a clear description of the agriculture practices we are following today. Permaculture is devoted to "care for earth, care for people, and sharing the surplus." It is a new fruit of the farm, but agriculture is one of our roots.

However, our deepest roots can be found in the Gospels, in particular the Sermon on the Mount, and from Acts of the Apostles:

> All the believers were together. They held all things in common. They were selling their property and possessions, and were distributing them to everyone according to each one's need. Every day they continued together in the temple. They broke bread in their houses. They shared food with gladness and in simplicity of heart. They praised God and had favor among all the people.

From 1942 to 1993, through many ups and downs, the community remained faithful to the vision of the early church and survived. Then there began a sojourn from that founding impetus that brought Koinonia nearer to extinction more than any bombs, bullets or boycotts of its early years. This detour ended in 2005 when a small band of people committed to return together to the communal structure.

Where to start in rebuilding a community? Beginning in 1942, Koinonia's mission was to live a way of life rooted in the Gospel and, inevitably, out of this shared life would come service to others. What we found at the heart of that beginning was the effort to simply be a good neighbor. The Jordans and Englands and those who came after them took "love your neighbor as yourself" as a command that required intention and action.

This notion of being firmly rooted in the Scripture and being in relationship with and loving our neighbor sounded like a good place to start for us as well. Those early Koinonians farmed, provided hospitality and offered an internship or discipleship school experience. They introduced new and effective ways of growing food. They welcomed whoever showed up regardless of race, faith, no faith, education or socio-economic background and shared food, shelter and fellowship with them. The internship was a period of immersion in this experiment in Christian living, an experience in living this very intentional way of life. These three activities are at the core of our life today.

But as we began this restart of the communal way of life at Koinonia, we also soon became aware of something else. As we looked at the roots and learned the history, we realized we had a responsibility that Clarence and Florence Jordan and Martin and Mabel England did not have when they founded the community. We had the responsibility to tell their story and the story of all those who came before us. And what a story it is. And what fruit it bore. We also had the opportunity to share with folks about all the good works that had come forth from or been inspired by Clarence and Koinonia.

Even more, though, we celebrated the obligation to disseminate Clarence Jordan's words, wisdom and wit. They are some of the best spiritual food we know. He continues to inspire and encourage us as we journey in God's kingdom and we cherish this chance to expose others to that same inspiration and encouragement that you have found in *Roots in the Cotton Patch* and *Fruits of the Cotton Patch*.

Much of what you have read in these two volumes is about our history, but the roots continue to grow deeper and there is much new fruit. One of the many life-giving experiences for us today is what you read in Jonathan Wilson-Hartgrove's chapter entitled "The Kingdom is like Kudzu: Koinonia Farm and a New Monasticism in America." We hope our call to live a simpler, gentler way of life serves as a demonstration plot for a way of life that is truly possible. As Jonathan stated, "If Clarence Jordan taught us anything, he taught that our task is to translate God's news into our own time and place. We do this, like Jesus, by enfleshing the message—turning words into deeds by the work of our hands and the grace of God, one day at

Afterword

a time, in scorn of the consequences. The essential thing is the demonstration plot. People need to see what God's movement looks like in practice. It is indeed, the gospel in blue jeans."

In our living, we still tear down walls as Shane Claiborne shares in his chapter. We do not choose to tear down those walls with aggressive rhetoric, with bombs, bullets and boycott of others, but rather we respond to the needs and challenges of the time with thoughtful action rooted in prayer. Or so we hope.

Today our life continues to generate stories and to bear fruit, but we are committed to honoring our past, honoring those who came before us. This collection of writings from the keynote addresses and seminars of the 2012 Clarence Jordan Symposium is one of the efforts to meet the responsibility to share the story and spread the wisdom. We pray that they have fed you spiritually.

To contact Koinonia Farm write us at 1324 GA Hwy 49 S, Americus, GA 31719, visit our Web site at koinoniafarm.org or call us at (229) 924-0391. Y'all come!

Bren Dubay
Koinonia Farm
2013

Celebrating the Life and Ministry of Clarence Jordan

A Working Bibliography

G. W. Carlson

The following bibliography is designed to allow the user an opportunity to develop a broader context for understanding the life and ministry of Clarence Jordan and the Koinonia Farm experiment. It is condensed from a larger bibliographical work that is more inclusive and provides materials on contemporary use of the Clarence Jordan story in today's church.

Besides the archives at Koinonia there are two important collections of materials on Clarence Jordan and Koinonia at the Hargrett Rare Book and Manuscript Library, University of Georgia in Athens, Georgia and Southern Baptist Archives in Nashville, Tennessee. The libraries at Southern Baptist Theological Seminary and Bethel Seminary have substantial collections of Clarence Jordan materials. Especially of interest is the collection of Clarence Jordan speeches and interviews.

Biographical and Historical Study of Clarence Jordan, Millard Fuller and Koinonia Farm

"According to Clarence." *Newsweek* February 26, 1968, 61.

Armstrong, O. K., and Marjorie Armstrong. "Clarence Jordan and Koinonia," in *The Baptists in America* New York: Doubleday, 1979, 377–79.

Barnette, Henlee H. *Clarence Jordan: Turning Dreams into Deeds* Macon, Georgia: Smyth and Helwys, 1992.
———. "Southern Baptist Seminary and the Civil Rights Movement: From 1859–1952." *Review and Expositor* vol. 93, Winter 1996, 77–126 (check dates Vol. 90, No. 4, Fall 1993, 531–50).
Blau, Eleanor. "30-Year Old Christian Commune in Georgia Thrives After Adversity." *New York Times* May 27, 1972.
Boers, Arthur. "The Prophet or the President." *The Other Side* January/February 1988. 32–36.
Bryan, G. McLeod. "Clarence Jordan, 1912–1969" in *Voices in the Wilderness* Atlanta, Georgia: Mercer Press, 1999, 53–76.
———. "Theology in Overalls" *Sojourners* Vol. 8, No. 12, December 1979, 10–11.
Campbell, Will D. "Where There's So Much Smoke" *Sojourners* Vol. 8, No. 12, December 1979, 19.
Carter, Jimmy. "Introduction" *Living Faith* New York: Three Rivers Press, 1996, 5–7.
———. "Riding Freely" in *Sources of Strength* New York: Times Book, 1997, 218–221.
Castle, David. "A Brief History of Koinonia: The Post-Jordan Years: 1970–2007" *Koinonia Partners, Inc,* Americus, Georgia, 2007.
Chancey, Andrew S. "A Demonstration Plot for the Kingdom of God: The Establishment and Early Years of Koinonia Farm" *Georgia Historical Quarterly* Vol. 75. No. 2, 1991, 321–353.
———. "Clarence Jordan (1912–1969)" *The New Georgia Encyclopedia* March 11, 2005.
———. "Koinonia Farm" *The New Georgia Encyclopedia* March 26, 2009.
———. "Koinonia in the '90s" *The Christian Century* October 14, 1992, 892–894.
———. "Race, Religion, and Agricultural Reform: The Communal Vision of Koinonia Farm" in *Georgia in Black and White: Explorations in the Race Relations of a Southern State, 1865–1950* (edited by John C. Inscoe) Athens, Georgia: University of Georgia Press, 1994.
Claiborne, Shane (et. al.). "October 29–Clarence Jordan" in *Common Prayer* Grand Rapids, Michigan: Zondervan, 2010, 495–497.
Coble, Ann Louise. *Cotton Patch for the Kingdom* Scottdale, Pennsylvania: Herald Press, 2002. Vol. 111, No. 21, July 13, 1994, 681.
———. "Cotton Patch Justice, Cotton Patch Peace: The Sermon on the Mount in the Teachings and Practices of Clarence Jordan" in *Theology and The New Histories* (edited by Gary Macy) New York: Orbis Books, 1998, 202–211.
Day, Dorothy. "Fear in Our Time" The Catholic Worker April 1968, 5,7.
———. "On Pilgrimage – May 1957" *The Catholic Worker* May 1957, 3,6.
Downing, Frederick L. "Rewriting the Cultural Myths: Clarence Jordan and the Cotton Patch Gospels" *Society of Biblical Literature*, 2011.
Dubay, Bren. "Koinonia: An Intentional Christian Community" *Koinonia Farm Chronicle,* Vol. 3, No. 1, Spring 2010, 2.
———. "Koinonia 70 Years Later: 1942–2012" *Koinonia Farm Chronicle* Vol. 4, No.. 1, Spring 2011, 1.
———. "Sink into Cynicism or Soar into Hope?" in *Cynicism and Hope* (edited by Meg E. Cox) Eugene, Oregon: Wipf and Stock, 2008, 65–71.
Gentry, Jerry. "Koinonia Turns Fifty" *Southern Exposure* Vol. XX, No. 2, Summer 1992, 58–63.

Harding, Rosemarie and Rachel Harding. "Radical Hospitality" *Sojourners* Vol. 32, No. 4, July-August 2003, 42–46.

Harding, Rosemarie and Vincent Harding. "Forward the Dawn" *Sojourners* Vol. 13, No. 13, April 1984, 24–25.

Harding, Rosemary Freeney as told to Rachel E. Harding. "There was a Tree in Starksville" *Sojourners*February 2012.

Harding, Vincent. *Hope and History* Maryknoll, New York: Orbis, 1990, 11–12, 205–209.

———. "In The Company of the Faithful: Journeying Toward the Promised Land" *Sojourners* Vol. 14, No. 5, May 1985, 14–21.

Hawkins, Mel. "A Faithful Remnant: Southern White Supporters of the Civil Rights Movement" *EthicsDaily.com* January 14, 2002.

Hearne, Joshua. "Clarence Jordan, Farmer, Founder of Koinonia Farm, Opponent of the Status Quo" *Telling the Stories that Matter* October 27, 2009.

Ho, Esther Mohler. "Koinonia Farm" Church Advocate February 1967, 5–7,11,15.

Hollyday, Joyce. "A Scandalous Life of Faith" *Sojourners* Vol. 8, No. 12, December 1979.

———. "Clarence Jordan: Theologian in Overalls" in *Cloud of Witnesses* (Edited by Jim Wallis and Joyce Hollyday) Maryknoll, New York: Orbis, 1991, 68–72.

———. "The Dream That Has Endured: Clarence Jordan and Koinonia" *Sojourners* Vol. 8, No. 12, December 1979.

Jordan, Jim. "Growing Up at Koinonia" *Christianity Today* March 9, 2005.

Kennedy, John W. "Hard Times Down on the Farm" *Christianity Today* January 9, 1995, 58–59.

K'Meyer, Tracy Elaine. *Interracialism and Christian Community in the Postwar South* Charlottesville: University Press of Virginia, 1997.

———. "'What Koinonia was all about' : The Role of Memory in a Changing Community" *The Oral History Review* Summer 1997, Vol. 24, No. 1. 1–22.

"Koinonia Farm." *The New Georgia Encyclopedia* Georgia Humanities Council and the University of Georgia Press March 26, 2009.

"Koinonians Seek to Follow Way of Life 'Jesus Taught." *Ebony* July 1957, 51–52.

Lee, Dallas. *The Cotton Patch Evidence: The Story of Clarence Jordan and the Koinonia Farm Experiment* New York: Harper and Row, 1971.

Lee, Rhonda Mawhood. "Admit Guilt–and Tell the Truth": The Louisville Fellowship of Reconciliations Struggle with Pacifism and Racial Justice, 1941-1945 *Journal of Southern History* May 1, 2010, 15, .Lee, Robert "The Crisis at Koinonia" *Christian Century* November 7, 1956, 1290–1291.

Lull, Howard W. "Koinonia Updated" Christian Century October 13, 1976, 868–872.

Marsh, Charles. "Charles Marsh Recounts Clarence Jordan's Conversion Experience That Led Him to Struggle Against Segregation in the Jim Crow South" *The Project of Lived Theology* 2010.

———. "In the Fields of the Lord: The God Movement in South Georgia" in *The Beloved Community* New York: Basic Books, 2005, 51–86.

———. "Work of Faith" *Christianity Today* February 23, 2005.

McClendon, Jr., James Wm. "The Theory Tested: Clarence Jordan–Radical in Community" in *Biography as Theology* Nashville, Tennessee: Abingdon, Press, 1974, 112–139.

McDowell, Edward. "Introduction" The Cotton Patch Version of Hebrews and the General Epistles, The Cotton Patch Gospel Koinonia Partners, 1973.

McNeely, Jack. "Making a Difference: Dubay Ready to Lead Koinonia Through Rebirth" *Americus Times-Recorder* Americus, Georgia, May 7, 2004.

Moore, Amanda. "Faith is the Life Based on Unseen Realities: Celebrating the Spirit of Clarence Jordan" *Koinonia Farm Chronicle*, Vol. 2, No. 2, Fall 2009, 1,3.

Mosley, Don and Joyce Hollyday. "Come, Ye Disconsolate" *Sojourners* July-August 1996, vol. 25, No. 4, 22–25.

Nelson, Jr. Claud. "Why We Are 'Withdrawing from the World'" *Motive* March 1953, 11–14.

Page, Dan. "Martin and Mabel" *Baptists Today* December 2004

Pitzer, D. E. "Jordan, Clarence (1912–1969) in *Dictionary of Baptists in America* (edited by Bill J. Leonard) Downers Grove, Illinois: InterVarsity Press, 1994, 157–158.

"Religion: Embattled Fellowship Farm." *Time* September 17, 1956.

"Rev. Clarence L. Jordan Dead; Led Interracial Farm Project." *New York Times* October 31, 1969.

Shurden, Walter B. "Southern Seminary in the Life of the Southern Baptist Convention" *Review and Expositor* Vol. LXXXI, No. 4, Fall 1984, 393–406.

Simmons, Paul D. "The Legacy of Clarence and Florence Jordan (address given on the occasion giving The Clarence Jordan Award to Rev. Lincoln Bingham for his exemplary Christian service in Louisville and Jefferson County. The recognition was established by the Long Run Baptist Association), 1992.

Snider, P. Joel. *The Cotton Patch Gospel: The Proclamation of Clarence Jordan* Lanham, MD: University Press of America, 1985.

Snider, Joel. "Hearing Parables in the Patch" *Christian Reflections* Center for Christian Ethics at Baylor University, 2006, 80–87.

Stricklin, David. "Clarence Jordan (1912–1969), Jasper Martin England (1901–1989) and Millard Fuller(1935-) Koinonia Farm: Epicenter for Social Change" in *Twentieth-Century Shapers of Baptist Social Ethics* (edited by Larry L. McSwain) Macon Georgia: Mercer University Press,2008, 163–184.

———. *A Genealogy of Dissent: Southern Baptist Protest in the Twentieth Century* Lexington, Kentucky: The University Press of Kentucky, 1999.

Strong, Douglas M. "Clarence Jordan (1912–1969): Creator of the 'Cotton Patch Gospel:' Building Biblical Community" *They Walked in the Spirit: Personal Faith and Social Action in America* Louisville, Kentucky: Westminster John Knox Press, 1997, 91–106.

Tillman, William M. "Clarence Jordan: Cotton Patch Prophet (1912–1969)" in *Baptist Prophets: Their Lives and Contributions* Brentwood, Tennessee: Baptist History and Heritage Society, 2006, 20–22.

Weiner, Kay N. (editor) *Koinonia Remembered* Americus, Georgia: Koinonia Partners, 1992.

York, Tripp. "Clarence Jordan's Fellowship" in *Living on Hope While Living in Babylon* Eugene, Oregon: Wipf and Stock, 2009, 60–80.

Clarence Jordan's Writings and Speeches

Hollyday, Joyce and Clarence Jordan. *Essential Writings* Maryknoll, New York: Orbis Books, 2003.

Jordan, Clarence. "As You Want People to Act Toward You" *The Church Advocate*, September 1967, 8–9.

———. "The Christian Community in the South" *Journal of Religious Thought* Vo. 14, No. 1, Autumn-Winter 1956–1957, 27–36.

———. *Clarence Jordan's Cotton Patch Gospel: The Complete Collection* Macon, Georgia: Smyth and Helwys, 2012.

———. *The Cotton Patch Version of Hebrews and the General Epistles* New York: Association Press, 1973.

———. *The Cotton Patch Version of Luke and Acts* Piscataway, N. J.: New Century Publishers, 1969.

———. *The Cotton Patch Version of Matthew and John* New York: Association Press, 1970.

———. "Dear President Eisenhower" January 22, 1957.

———. "Draft the Boys at 65" *Bruderhof Communities* 2004.

———. "The Good Samaritan" Mennonite Life January 1967, 17–18.

———. "Here is the Church" Peace and Justice Home Page Koinonia Partners.

———. "Impractical Christianity" *Sunday School Young Peoples' Quarterly* Third Quarter 1948, 2.

———. "In the Land of Great Violence" *The Mennonite* Vol. 25, May 1965, 353.

———. "Is It an Impossible Job?" *Young People* Vol. 12, August 1956, 9–10.

———. "Is Non-Violence Enough?" *Baptist Leader* February 1964, 12–13.

———. "Jesus and Possessions" in *Kingdom Building: Essays from the Grassroots of Habitat* (edited by Robert William Stevens and David Johnson Rowe) Americus, Georgia: Habitat for Humanity, 1984.

———. "Learn to Take It on the Chin" *The Church Advocate* August 1966, 8–9.

———. *The Letter to God's People in Washington or Romans* Americus, Georgia: Koinonia Farm, 1968.

———. *Letters to God's People in Columbus (Colossians) and Selma (I and II Thessalonians): In the Koinonia Cotton Patch Version* Americus, Georgia, Koinonia Publications, 1967.

———. "Letter to President Eisenhower" January 22, 1957.

———. "Love Your Enemies" *Post-American* Vol. 2, May-June 1972, 4–5.

———. "The Meaning of Christian Fellowship" *Prophetic Religion* Vol. 7, Spring 1946, 3–6.

———. "The Meaning of Thanatos and Nekros in the Epistles of Paul" Unpublished Doctoral Dissertation, Southern Baptist Theological Seminary Louisville, Kentucky, 1938.

———. "One Jesus for Another" *Christian Living* October 1965, 20–22.

———. "A Parable of No Violence, Some Violence, and Great Violence" *Town and County Church* November-December 1965, .9.

———. "Peace and Brotherhood" *Koinonia Peace and Justice* Baptist Peace Fellowship, Detroit Michigan, May 19, 1963.

———. "A Personal Letter to Friends of Koinonia Farm" *The Church Advocate* July 1969, 12–13.

———. *Practical Religion or, the Sermon on the Mount and the Epistle of James in the Koinonia Cotton Patch Version* Americus, Georgia: Koinonia Farm, 1964.

———. "Racial Frontiers" *Baptist Student* November 1941, 6–7.

———. "The Rich Farmer" *The Presbyterian Outlook* March 27, 1967, 4.

———. "The Sound of a Dove" *Town and Country Church* 1961, 16.

———. *The Substance of Faith and Other Cotton Patch Sermons* (edited by Dallas Lee) Eugene, Oregon: Cascade Books, 2005.

———. *Sermon on the Mount* Valley Forge, Pennsylvania: Judson Press, 1952.

———. "Things New and Old" in *Peace and Nonviolence* (edited by Edward Guinan) New York: Paulist Press, 1973, 114–120.
———. "When Jesus Came to Georgia" *The Church Advocate* February 1967, 8–9.
———. "Why Study the Bible?" Philadelphia: Baptist Youth Fellowship, 1953.
Jordan, Clarence and Bill Lane Doulos. *Cotton Patch Parables of Liberation* Scottdale, Pennsylvania: Herald Press, 1976.

Clarence Jordan and Friends Speeches and Interviews

Included are examples of Clarence Jordan's speeches or presentations about Clarence Jordan and Koinonia Farm. Materials listed include places where the items can be found. Materials that can be purchased from the Koinonia catalog are marked with the letter "K." Some items can also be found in Southern Baptist Theological Seminary Library (SBTS) and Bethel Seminary (BS).

Records

Jordan, Clarence. "The Great Banquet and Other Parables" Tiskilwa, Illinois: Koinonia Records, nd. (BS)
———. "Jesus the Rebel and Jesus and Possessions" Evanston, Illinois: Koinonia Records, nd.
———. "Metamorphosis and Love Your Enemies" Evanston, Illinois: Koinonia Records, nd.
———. "The Rich Man and Lazarus and Other Parables retold for Our Times" Evanston, Illinois: Koinonia Records, nd. (BS)
———. "Judas" Evanston, Illinois: Koinonia Records, nd.

Tapes/CDs

Jordan, Clarence. "Christian Pacifism/Draft the Boys at 65" (CD/K)
———. "Christians Under Pressure" Americus, Georgia: Koinonia Records. (3 cassettes) (BS)
———. "The Cotton Patch Parables: A Bible Study for Thinking Christians" (4 CD set with study guide) (CD/K)
———. "Episodes from Acts" Americus, Georgia: Koinonia Records (2 cassettes) (BS)
———. "Great Banquet/Angry Banker and Rich Farmer/Buried Treasure" Americus, Georgia: Koinonia Partners, nd. (1 cassette) (BS)
———. "Incarnating Brotherhood" Americus, Georgia: Koinonia Records (1 cassette) (BS)
———. "Jesus the Rebel and Jesus and Possessions" Americus, Georgia: Koinonia Partners, nd.(1 cassette) (BS)

Celebrating the Life and Ministry of Clarence Jordan

———. "Judas and The Man from Gadera" Americus, Georgia: Koinonia Partners, nd. (1 cassette) (BS)
———. "Metamorphosis and Love Your Enemies" Americus, Georgia: Koinonia Partners, nd. (1 Cassette) (BS)
———. "The Koinonia Story" Americus, Georgia: Koinonia Partners nd. (CD/K)
———. "Power from Parables" Americus, Georgia: Koinonia Records. (4 cassettes) (BS)
———. "The Prodigal Son, Rich Man and Lazarus, and The Good Samaritan" Americus, Georgia: Koinonia Partners, nd. (1 cassette) (BS)
———. "Man of Faith: Selections from Jordan's Sermons and Lectures" Americus, Georgia: Koinonia Partners, nd.
———. "The Sabbath as a Way of Life" Americus, Georgia: Koinonia Records. (1 cassette) (BS)
———. "Living the Sermon on the Mount" (recorded at the American Baptist Conference Center in Green Lake Wisconsin. (cassette) (BS)
———. "Substance of Faith" Americus, Georgia: Koinonia Records (1 cassette) (BS)
Morrison, Scott. "Clarence Jordan Interview" Americus, Georgia: Koinonia Partners, nd. (CD/K)

DVD's and VHS and Relevant Supporting Materials

Briars in the Cottonpatch: The Story of Koinonia Farm Cotton Patch Productions, 2003. (DVD/K)
Cotton Patch Gospel (Tom Key) Bridgestone Productions, 1988. (DVD/K)
Cotton Patch Gospel (Tom Key) (CD/K)
Staggs, Al "Clarence Jordan and the God Movement" (DVD/K)
———. "Role Models for Walking the Talk in the 21st Century." *American Baptist News Service,* July 1, 2009.
Synopisis of "Briars in the Cotton Patch." *Georgia Public Broadcasting,* February 2005.
"Tom Key Looks Back." *Dramatic Publishing* 2004.
Westmoreland-White, Michael L. "Al Staggs: Baptist Minister and Acts for the Kingdom" *Levellers* July 31, 2007.

Audiovisual materials on Clarence Jordan at Southern Baptist Theological Seminary Library, Bethel Seminary Library and Other Sites

Barnette, Henlee H. and Frank Stagg. "Chapel Address, November 19, 1969, : Memorial Service for Clarence Jordan" Southern Baptist Theological Seminary, Louisville, Kentucky (audiobook Reel-to-reel) (SBTS)
Barnette, Henlee H. "Chapel Address" April 6–7, 1982" (Louisville, Kentucky: Southern Baptist Theological Seminary, 1982. (cassette) (SBTS)
———. "Clarence Jordan" March 13, 1984 Ethics Luncheon Southern Baptist Theological Seminary 9 (cassette) (SBTS)

Finlator, William Wallace. "Chapel Address: Clarence Jordan and the Bible" April 19, 1983, (Recorded in Alumni Memorial Chapel, Southern Baptist Theological Seminary. (cassette) (SBTS)

———. "Clarence Jordan and Economic Issues" April 20, 1983, Chapel Address Southern Baptist Theological Seminary (cassette) (SBTS)

Jamison, Gayla. "Enough to Share a Portrait of Koinonia Farm 1983 Southern Baptist Theological Seminary. (video) (SBTS)

Jordan, Clarence. "Ancient Men with a Modern Twist" Bible Lectures February 2-5, 1969 (Bethel College, Kansas) (cassette)

———. "Chapel Address: The Humanity of God," October 2, 1968, Southern Baptist Theological Seminary, Louisville, Kentucky) (cassette) (SBTS)

———. "Chapel Address, 1983, April. 20: Clarence Jordan and Economic Issues" (recorded in Alumni Memorial Chapel, Southern Baptist Theological Seminary) (cassette) (SBTS)

———. "Christianity as a Movement" (audio mp3 file) *Peace and Justice Home Page* Koinonia Partners.

———. "Classroom Lecture" October 2, 1968 (recorded at Southern Baptist Theological Seminary) (cassette) (SBTS)

———. "Lecture: On Nonviolence" October 1, 1968 Southern Baptist Theological Seminary. (SBTS)

———. "Power in the Parables" Bible Lectures (audio) Bethel College, Kansas, February 2-5, 1969.

———. "Spiritual Discipline" 1959 Southern Baptist Theological Seminary. (SBTS)

Jordan, Florence "Koinonia Today: With Discussion Questions"), 1982-1983. (cassette) (recorded at Southern Baptist Theological Seminary) (SBTS)

———. "Classroom Lecture" April 19, 1983, Southern Baptist Theological Seminary. (SBTS)

———. "Classroom Lecture" May 3, 1974 Southern Baptist Theological Seminary (SBTS)

Pratt, Kris. "Justice in the Cotton Patch: Clarence Jordan on Economic and Racial Justice" CBGNC General Assembly, March 25, 2011. (audio recording)

Ragsdale, Vicki. "Interview of Florence Jordan" Recorded in the Southern Baptist Theological Seminary Television Studio, March 18, 1986. (video) (SBTS)

Simmons, Paul D., Dale Moody and W. Peyton Thurman. "Interviews About Clarence Jordan: Paul Simmons interviews Dale Moody and Peyton Thurman About the life of Clarence Jordan and His Work as Founder of Koinonia Farms" Recorded in the Southern Baptist Theological Seminary Television Studio, 1980. (video) (SBTS)

Thurman, William Peyton, Dale Moody, and Paul D. Simmons. "Chapel Address, April 29, 1981,Reflections on Clarence Jordan" (audiobook cassette) Alumni Memorial Chapel, Southern Baptist Theological Seminary (SBTS)

Selective Habitat for Humanity and Millard and Linda Fuller Writings and Speeches

Baggett, Jerome P. *Habitat for Humanity: Building Private Homes, Building Public Religion* Philadelphia: Temple University Press, 1960.

Bryant, John Hope. "A Legend, Habitat for Humanity Founder Millard Fuller Dies" *johnhopebryant.com*February 5, 2009. (good chronology)

Carter, Jimmy. "Interview with Millard Fuller" *ChristianEthicsToday* December 1995, Issue 4, 6.

Clemens, Steve. "Remembering Millard: My Reminiscing About Millard Fuller" *FullerCenter.org*, March 19, 2009.

"A Conversation with Millard Fuller" *Single Adult Ministries Journal* March 1998, 9-11.

Frykholm, Amy. "One House At a Time" *Christian Century* December 16, 2008, 10-11.

Fuller, Millard. *Beyond the American Dream* Macon, Georgia: Smyth and Helwys, 2010.

———. *Building Materials for Life, Volume I* Macon, Georgia: Smyth and Helwys, 2002.

———. *Building Materials for Life Volume II* Macon, Georgia: Smyth and Helwys, 2004.

———. *Building Materials for Life Volume III* Macon, Georgia: Smyth and Helwys.2007.

———. *Bokotola* New York: Association Press, 1977.

——— *The Excitement is Building* Waco, Texas: Word Publishing, 1990.

———. "A House is a Sermon of Christ" *Eternity* September 1997, 44-45.

———. "An Interview with Millard Fuller" Christian Ethics Today Vol. 4, December 27, 2010.

———. (with Diane Scott) *Love in the Mortar Joints* Piscataway, New Jersey: New Century Publishers, 1980.

———. *More Than Houses: How Habitat for Humanity is Transforming Lives and Neighborhoods* Waco, Texas: Word Inc., 2000.

———. *No More Shacks*! Waco, Texas: Word Books, 1986.

———. "Quiet Heroes: Building a Life" *Christian Networks Journal* Winter 2002, 14-15.

———. *A Simple, Decent Place to Live: The Building Realization of Habitat for Humanity* Dallas, Texas: Word Publishers, 1995.

———. *Theology of the Hammer* Macon, Georgia: Smyth and Helwys, 1994.

Fuller, Millard and Linda Fuller. *The Excitement is Building* Dallas: Word Publishing, 1990.

Gailard, Frye. *If I Were a Carpenter: Twenty Years of Habitat for Humanity* John F. Blair, 1996.

Goodrich, Chris. *Faith is a Verb* Gimlet Eyes Books, 2005.

Hayes, Kathleen. "Interview with Millard Fuller" *Other Side* January 1986, 12-15.

Hinson, David and Justin Miller. *Designed for Habitat* London: Routledge, 2012.

Korthase, Sherry C. "Millard Fuller (1935-2009)" *The New Georgia Encyclopedia* February 5, 2009.

Lewis, Gregg. "Linda and Millard Fuller" *Marriage Partnership* Spring 1990, 38-40.

Lyman-Barner, Kirk. "What the Poor Need is Not Charity, But Capital. So, What Do the Rich Need? *The Fuller Center* January 28, 2011.

Martin, Douglas "Millard Fuller, 74, Who Founded Habitat for Humanity, Is Dead" *New York Times* February 4, 2009, 28.

Maudlin, Michael. "God's Contractor" *Christianity Today* June 14, 1999. 44-47.

"Millard Fuller, 1935-2009:Habitat Founder Remembered as Visionary." *Christian Century* March 10, 2009, 17.

Pierce, John. "Master Builder for God: Remembered Simply" *Baptists Today* February 4, 2009.

———. "Millard, Socks and the Taser Guy." *Baptists Today* October 26, 2009.

Shor, Fran. "Hammerin' on Heavens Door" *New Politics* Winter 2008, 65-70.

Stafford, Tim. "How to Build Homes Without Putting Up Walls" *Christianity Today* June 10, 2002.

Stelten, Gene G. *Thanks Mom! A Collection of Stories and Artwork to Benefit Habitat for Humanity* Peachtree Press, 1999.

Schwartz, Bob. "Millard Fuller and Clarence Jordan" *Religion Report* February 4, 2009.

Starling, Kelly. "Habitat for Humanity" *Ebony* November 1997, 200–207.

Vande Koppelle, Robert P. *The Invisible Mountain: A Journey of Faith* Eugene, Oregon: Wipf and Stock, 2010.

Willimon, William H. "Millard Fuller's Theology of the Hammer" *Christian Century* October 5, 1988, 862–863.

Youngs, Bettie B. *The House That Love Built* Charlottesville, Virginia: Hampton Road Publishing, 2007.

Materials and Responses to Clarence Jordan Symposium

Allen, Bob. "Jimmy Carter fetes Clarence Jordan" *abpnews* October 11, 2012.

———. "Koinonia Farms Plans Clarence Jordan Symposium" *abpnews* July 31, 2012.

Carey, Greg. "Recalling Clarence Jordan, Radical Disciple" *huffingtonpost.com* June 3, 2012.

Carlson, G. W. "Clarence Jordan: Celebrating a Conscientious Christian Dissenter" *The Pietist Schoolman* August 16, 2012.

———. "Reflections on the Clarence Jordan Symposium" *The Pietist Schoolman*, December 20, 2012.

Cep, Casey N. "Christ in the Cotton Patch: Clarence Jordan and the Koinonia Farm" *huffingtonpost.com*November 19, 2012.

Claiborne, Shane. "Happy Birthday Clarence!" *redletterchristians.org* July 28, 2012.

Claiborne, Shane and Jonathan Wilson-Hartgrove. "Remembering Clarence Jordan" Vimeo October 5, 2012.

"Clarence Jordan: The Man Who Inspired the Fullers' Affordable Housing Movement" *Fuller Center for Housing* July 27, 2012.

Clemens, Steve. "Remembering Clarence Jordan on 100 Anniversary of His Birth" *Mennonista* 2012.

Fossum, Christy. "Koinonia Farm and Clarence Jordan Celebration" sundaybysunday withchristy.blogspot.com October 4, 2012.

Gatlin, Joe. "All Things in Common" *Habitat World* August 2012.

Gregg, Carl. "From Independence Day to Interdependence" *patheos.com* July 3, 2012.

Harvey, Paul. "Interracialism and Christian Community in the Postwar South: Clarence Jordan, Southern Baptist Visionary" *usreligion.blogspotcom* August 12, 2012.

Hearne, Joshua. "Clarence Jordan, Farmer, Founder of Koinonia Farm, Opponent of the Status Quo" *Telling Stories that Matter* October 27, 2012.

Hodges, Sam. "The Enduring Influence of Clarence Jordan" the *United Methodist Reporter* September 15, 2012.

Johnson, Chris. "Clarence Jordan at 100: An Influential Soul" *Fuller Center for Housing* 2012.

———. "Clarence Jordan: The Man Who Inspired the Fullers' Affordable Housing Movement" *The Fuller Center*, July 27, 2012.

———. "Simple Way's Shane Claiborne brings Fuller Center to Philadelphia" *Fuller Center for Housing* November 30, 2012.

Kaylor, Brian. "Happy Birthday Clarence" *blog.briankaylor.com* July 29, 2012.

Kohls, Gary G. "Clarence Jordan, Conscientious Objector to War and Killing: More Lessons From the History of American Fascism, Racism, Militarism, and Economic Oppression" *duluthreader.com*. June 22, 2012.

Lyman-Barner, Kirk. "Clarence Never Said: 'Nothing Can Be Done'" *koinonia 2012celebration.org* July 27, 2012.

———. *Koinonia Farm 2012 Celebration: Commemorative Program September 28–29, 2012* Americus, Georgia: A Koinonia Publication, 2012.

———. "A Ride on the Love Train" *The Fuller Center for Housing*, March 16, 2012.

McBrayer, Ronnie. "A Demonstration Plot: Remembering Clarence Jordan, Part 1 of 3" *blog.beliefnet.com* September 2012.

———. "Help Us Ship the Nuts Out of Georgia – Remembering Clarence Jordan, Part 2 of 3" *blog.beliefnet.com* September 2012.

———. "In Scorn of Consequences—Remembering Clarence Jordan, Party 3 of 3" *blog.beliefnet.com* September 2012.

Millstein, Ezra. "All Things in Common" *parliamentofreligions.org* September 19, 2012.

Nelson-Munson, Pamela. "Stripping Down to God" Ashland, Oregon: First United Methodist Church, October 14, 2012.

Pierce, John. "Loving Respect, Clear Disagreement" *Baptists Today* April 30, 2012.

———. "Vincent Harding: 'Keeper of a Story'" *Baptists Today* April 30, 2012.

Seat, Leroy. "Cotton Patch Saint Committed to Nonviolence" *ethicsdaily.com* August 1, 2012.

———. "In Praise of Clarence Jordan" *theviewfromthisseat.blogspotcom* July 30, 2012.

Shenk, Joanna. "A Farm for the Kingdom" *Mennonite World Review* July 9, 2012.

Staggs, Al. "Koinonia Farm 2012 Celebration" *Koinonia 2012* July 27, 2012.

Swartz, Ted. "The Clarence Jordan Symposium" *tedandcompany.com* 2012.

Umstattd, Scott. "Clarence Jordan and Martin Luther King Jr.: Meeting in Albany Georgia" *Briars Documentary* March 24, 2012.

Wilson-Hartgrove, Jonathan. "Clarence Jordan and God's Movement Today" *patheos.com* July 2, 2012.

———. "Hope for the Future in Our Radical Past" *patheos.com* October 1, 2012.

———. "21st Century Freedom Ride" *redletterchirstians.org* November 7, 2012.

———. "The Truth About Community" *patheos.com* January 7, 2013.

Wood, George P. "Clarence Jordan Never Said, 'Nothing Can Be Done.'" georgewood.com July 30, 2012.

Yoder, Kelli. "Looking for Heroes: Radical Activism Isn't Inspired at First Glance" *Mennonite World Review* October 29, 2012

Contributors

JIMMY CARTER (James Earl Carter, Jr.), thirty-ninth president of the United States, was born October 1, 1924, in the small farming town of Plains, Georgia, just fifteen minutes from Koinonia Farm. He served as President of the United States from 1977 to 1981. Significant foreign policy accomplishments of his administration included the Panama Canal treaties, the Camp David Accords, the treaty of peace between Egypt and Israel, the SALT II treaty with the Soviet Union, and the establishment of US diplomatic relations with the People's Republic of China. On the domestic side, the administration's achievements included a comprehensive energy program conducted by a new Department of Energy; major educational programs under a new Department of Education; and major environmental protection legislation. After leaving the Presidency, Carter became University Distinguished Professor at Emory University in Atlanta, and founded the Carter Center. He was awarded the Nobel Peace Prize in 2002 for his decades of untiring effort to find peaceful solutions to international conflicts, to advance democracy and human rights, and to promote economic and social development. President and Mrs. Rosalynn Carter have three sons, one daughter, twelve grandchildren, and six great-grandchildren. He is the author of twenty-five books, a long-time volunteer and supporter of Habitat for Humanity, and a Sunday school teacher at Maranatha Baptist Church, in Plains.

SHANE CLAIBORNE is one of the cofounders of the Simple Way, an intentional Christian community located in the inner city of Philadelphia, that has helped to birth and connect radical faith communities around the world. Much like Clarence Jordan, Shane lives a shared life in a community rooted in the gospel, and his service emerges from it. With tears and laughter, Shane Claiborne unveils the tragic messes we've made of our world and the tangible hope that another world is possible.

Contributors

JOE GATLIN has worked for Habitat for Humanity for more than twenty-five years, currently serving as the Director of Field Operations in Habitat International's US Area Office. He has worked with Habitat affiliates across the United States, assisting them in start-up, organizational growth, and mission and vision fulfillment and interpretation. He and his wife, Nancy, have been cofounders and pastors of Christian communities that grew out of communal households based in lower-income neighborhoods of Chicago and Waco, Texas. For the last seventeen years they have been part of Hope Fellowship in Waco, a member of the Shalom Mission Communities association. Joe has a seminary degree from Garrett-Evangelical Theological Seminary and a law degree from Loyola University. In 1968, when he was sixteen and trying to understand the implications of his Christian commitment in the context of the Vietnam War and a Southern Baptist church upbringing, Joe took note of Jesus' pacifism and the extraordinary life of the Jerusalem church in Acts 2. He was deeply moved when he read *The Cotton Patch Evidence* in the early 1970s, and has been blessed ever since to be part of what Clarence called the God Movement.

PHILIP GULLEY is a Quaker pastor and beloved writer and speaker from Danville, Indiana. An eclectic writer, Philip has published seventeen books, including the acclaimed *Harmony* series chronicling life in the eccentric Quaker community of Harmony, Indiana, and the best-selling *Porch Talk* series of inspirational and humorous essays. Gulley's memoir, *I Love You, Miss Huddleston: And Other Inappropriate Longings of My Indiana Childhood,* recounts his coming-of-age years in Danville. In addition, Philip and co-author James Mulholland describe their progressive worldview in their books, *If Grace Is True* and *If God Is Love,* followed by Philip's book *If the Church Were Christian.* In his most recently published book, *The Evolution of Faith: How God is Creating a Better Christianity*, Philip proposes a fresh direction for Christianity and articulates a Christianity that, while faithful to the priorities of Jesus, can help its adherents live happily, peacefully, and productively in our complex world.

DAVID ANDERSON HOOKER is an Associate Professor of conflict studies at Eastern Mennonite University. He also serves as Senior Fellow for Community Engagement Strategies at the University of Georgia's Fanning Institute for Public Service and Outreach. For more than thirty years David has been a mediator, facilitator, and community organizer. David has mediated over 500 cases and serves as Executive Assistant Pastor and Minister of Local and Global Outreach for First Congregational Church in Atlanta. He has worked throughout the United States and around the globe, focusing on issues of environmental justice, post-riot racial reconciliation, community development, democratization, and multiparty conflict resolution.

TOM KEY has served since 1995 as the Executive Artistic Director of Theatrical Outfit with the purpose to give dramatic voice to the spiritual themes of the American South. He has been a solo performer in demand across North America for more than two decades, including appearances of his *C. S. Lewis On Stage* and *The Revelation of John* at the John F. Kennedy Center for the Performing Arts, Lambs Theater Off Broadway, the Westwood Playhouse of Los Angeles, the Alliance Theater, Dallas Theater Center, Oxford University, Harvard University, and Yale University. With the late singer-songwriter Harry Chapin, Tom conceived and co-authored the off-Broadway musical hit *Cotton Patch Gospel*, still one of the most produced plays in the musical catalogue.

RONNIE MCBRAYER was born and raised in the foothills of the North Georgia Appalachians and claims he barely survived the fire and brimstone instruction of his hard-shell, Baptist-reared childhood. But in the great comedy of God, Ronnie has spent his adulthood in Christian ministry, preaching in and protesting against; loving and leaving; running away from and returning to the church. The faith he is trying to keep isn't in organized religion, however. It is in Jesus.

DAVID SNELL is a veteran of Habitat for Humanity leadership, serving in the field in the United States and in Mexico for ten years. He is the former director of Habitat Education Ministries and spent seven years as president of Habitat for Humanity Colorado. David was a cofounder of the Fuller Center for Housing and oversaw the formation and growth of new Fuller Center projects and partnerships as the Vice President for Programs. In that capacity he traveled extensively around the world. In February 2009, the board elected him to serve as the Fuller Center's second president after the death of founder Millard Fuller.

Contributors

AL STAGGS holds a B.A. from Hardin-Simmons University, an M.R.E. from Southwestern Baptist Theological Seminary, a Th.M. from Harvard Divinity School, and a Doctor of Ministry degree from Austin Presbyterian Theological Seminary. He also completed a year internship in Clinical Pastoral Education at Baylor University Medical Center in Dallas, Texas. In the spring of 1983 he was honored as a Charles E. Merrill Fellow at Harvard with major emphasis in Applied Theology, under the direction of Harvey Cox.

In 1992 **TED SWARTZ** graduated from seminary and began a ministry that took him, not to a pulpit in a congregation, but to audiences across the US and beyond. The first twenty years of this work included the creation of Ted and Lee TheaterWorks, with Lee Eshleman, and development of plays such as *Armadillo Shorts, Fish-Eyes, Creation Chronicles, Live at Jacob's Ladder,* and *DoveTale*. Since Lee's death in May, 2007, Ted has been writing and performing new plays with a number of other artists. Ted lives in the Shenandoah Valley of Virginia. Along with writing and acting, his loves include his wife, Sue; three sons, Eliot, Ian, and Derek; and new daughters-in-law, Katrina and Hannah—oh, and baseball.

For more than thirty years, **DR. DOLPHUS WEARY** has spoken on college campuses, in churches, seminaries, and conferences around the country. "I believe that God has given me two passions, a passion for racial unity in the body of Christ and to minister to those who are poor in Mississippi and around the country." Currently Dolphus serves as the President of Rural Education and Leadership (R.E.A.L.) Christian Foundation (a foundation connecting economic and technical resources with rural Christian ministries) and as a consultant for Mission Mississippi (a racial reconciliation ministry that encourages unity within the body of Christ). Dolphus served on the Board of Directors at Koinonia Farm during the period when Partnership Housing was first launched.

WAYNE WEISEMAN is certified by the Permaculture Institute of Australia and the Worldwide Permaculture Network as an instructor of the Permaculture Design Certificate Course. He is also certified by the American Institute of Architecture (AIA) and the American Society of Landscape

Architects (ASLA) to teach continuing education in permaculture to licensed architects and landscape architects. Wayne is Director of The Permaculture Project LLC and Permaculture Design-Build Collaborative LLC, a full-service, international consulting and educational businesses promoting the ideas of eco-agriculture, renewable energy resources and eco-construction methods. For many years he managed a land-based, self-reliant community project combining organic crop/food production, ecologically built shelter, renewable energy, and appropriate technologies. Wayne sits on the board of Mindful Generations, a non-profit guild of educators creating economic and community development in Third World countries through small-scale agriculture training programs.

Jonathan Wilson-Hartgrove is author of ten books, a new monastic, and sought-after speaker. A native of North Carolina, he is a graduate of Eastern University and Duke Divinity School. Shortly before the United States began bombing Iraq in 2003, Jonathan and his wife, Leah, traveled there as members of a Christian Peacemaker Team determined to tell Iraqis that American Christians did not all support the war. Their experiences became the subject of *To Baghdad and Beyond* (Cascade, 2005), which describes the couple's conversion to the "new monasticism." Jonathan is an Associate Minister at the historically black St. Johns Baptist Church, and is engaged in peacemaking and reconciliation efforts in Durham, North Carolina. The Rutba House, where Jonathan lives with his family and other friends, is a new monastic community that prays, eats, and lives together, welcoming neighbors and the homeless.

www.ingramcontent.com/pod-product-compliance
Lightning Source LLC
Chambersburg PA
CBHW022125160426
43197CB00009B/1152